A LOGIC OF EXPRESSIVE CHOICE

A LOGIC OF
EXPRESSIVE CHOICE

ALEXANDER A. SCHUESSLER

PRINCETON UNIVERSITY PRESS

PRINCETON AND LONDON

#43095818

Library of Congress Cataloging-in-Publication Data

Schuessler, Alexander A., 1965–
A logic of expressive choice / Alexander A. Schuessler.
p. cm.
Includes bibliographical references and index.
ISBN 0-691-00661-X (CL: alk. paper)
ISBN 0-691-00662-8 (paper: alk. paper)
1. Rational choice theory.   2. Voting.   3. Political participation.   I. Title.

HM495.S38 2000
301'.01—dc21   99-087372

This book has been composed in Palatino

The paper used in this publication meets the minimum requirements of ANSI/NISO
Z39.48-1992 (R 1997) (*Permanence of Paper*)

http://pup.princeton.edu

Printed in the United States of America

10 9 8 7 6 5 4 3 2 1

10 9 8 7 6 5 4 3 2 1
(pbk.)

For My Parents

Jede Geschichte ist eine Erfindung,
jedes Ich das sich ausspricht eine Geschichte
(Max Frisch)

CONTENTS

PREFACE

IN THIS BOOK I argue that many types of participation in collective activities—such as voting in large-scale elections and participating in the consumption of mass-produced goods—represent instances in which individuals express and reaffirm, to others and to themselves, who they are. Voters in American elections choose Democratic and Republican candidates, as this is how they themselves become or remain Democrats and Republicans. Consumers choose particular goods, and their choice in part is motivated by their understanding of what it means to be someone in possession of those goods. In such instances, the motivation that guides individuals' participation in these activities is one of *expressive attachment*: through their participation, these voters and consumers *express* who they are, and they *attach* to a collective that they feel is like them.

Since the 1950s, a growing number of social scientists in general and political scientists in particular have begun to model in incentive-driven or "economic" terms the political behavior of voters in elections, within interest groups, in citizen movements and demonstrations, and in a host of other political activities. In what has come to be known as rational choice theory, citizens are understood as outcome-oriented, rational individuals who allocate their own political resources (most notably their participation) in order to maximize strategically their impact on political outcomes they care about most. For example, they vote for candidates whose policy preferences are closest to their own, and they contribute to interest groups with a policy focus matching their own. These forms of political participation are meant to change the political world to match more closely the preferences of the respective participants. Although these analytical approaches arguably have been quite successful in helping political scientists predict how citizens will *choose* in elections and elsewhere, they have also been hounded by an inability to understand why citizens choose to *participate* in many of these types of activity in the first place. If, indeed, they are instrumentally rational individuals who participate in elections in order to secure a preferred outcome, then why do they participate at this level of politics in the first place? The probability of single-votedly determining the outcome of a large election, for example, is indistinguishable from zero. The electoral- outcome-related benefit of voting, consequently, is certain to be overwhelmed by the associated cost of participation in the election. It simply cannot therefore be rational (at least if the voter's reason for participating in the election is to have an effect on its outcome) to participate in large-scale voting.

This well-known puzzle, known as the paradox of participation, appears in all instances of political behavior wherein the outcome is determined by the behavior of a collective—or by "collective action." The larger that collective, the more paradoxical the participation of its members. Reactions among political economists to the problem of collective action have been threefold. Some have changed their understanding of incentives to force an explanation that it may still be rational to participate: for example, the source of payoffs may lie somewhere other than in the electoral outcome. You may care more about the fact that your participation will please your mother or your spouse than you do about the utter irrelevance of your participation in the world of national politics. Others have acknowledged the gravity of the problem and subsequently ignored the question of participation, or turnout, focusing instead only on the question of voter choice (where rational choice theory has been more successful). And a third group has argued that participation in large-scale collective action simply is guided by something other than instrumentally rational, outcome-oriented concerns. Instead, voting is to be understood as "emotional," "liturgical," "symbolic," or "expressive." Consequently, these theorists have argued that it is inappropriate to approach such behavior in terms of incentives or any other notions derived from neoclassical economics.

The approach in this book shares with this latter group of theorists the notion that participation in large-scale collective action often will be driven by citizens' expressive motivation. In addition, however, I argue that such expressively motivated action may carry its own system of incentives: in other words, it is in fact possible to identify a logic of expressive choice, much as we have been able to identify an instrumentally rational logic of collective action. Voters and consumers are motivated, at least in part, by a desire to gain and express an identity through their participation in voting and consumption. Political and product advertising campaigns, subsequently, are designed to entice these prospective participants by indicating to them *what it means*, expressively, to be a participant. This point is an obvious and long-familiar one to practitioners in marketing, and at least implicitly so to political scientists providing descriptive accounts of electoral campaigns. (In fact, as I show in this book, campaign managers have learned, and continue to learn, from practitioners in marketing how to focus their strategic energies on prospective participants' desires for expression.) Neither group of researchers, however, has formulated a cohesive theory of attachment and participation, nor has this expressive relationship between prospective participants and those eliciting their participation been captured by political economists seeking to model political participation formally.

The purpose of this book is threefold. First, it is to provide a theoretical microfoundation for expressively motivated participation in collective action. Here, rather than look toward neoclassical economics and game theory, I look toward schools in social theory and anthropology that have long held the foundational assumption that human behavior is expressive, symbolic, and interpretive. Unlike theorists of these schools, however, I do not claim that the social scientist's task, subsequently, should be to provide an interpretivist analysis. Scholars associated with interpretivist schools (of hermeneutics and semiotics initially, and of "postmodern" thought subsequently) tend to divide into those seeking to understand *what* social behavior expresses on the one hand and *how* it expresses on the other. To the extent that the approach in this book overlaps with theirs, it is decidedly with the philosophically more mundane but analytically more tractable question of *how* expressive value is generated, and how expressive motivated participation subsequently is elicited. Specifically, I do not seek to identify what it expresses for voters to vote for various candidates, but how such expressive relevance will in part depend on the actions of candidates, their campaigns, and other voters.

A second purpose of this book is to show how some of the insights of these social theorists lend themselves to being operationalized by drawing on simple tools provided by microeconomists of both the "price" and "game theory" variety. It is possible to define and explore "economies" of expressive incentives, and the purpose here is to provide a simple example of what one such economy might look like. In doing so, I identify two classes of actors—prospective participants (voters, consumers, interest group and campaign contributors, and so on) and producers of participation (campaign managers, political consultants, advertising practitioners, interest group leaders). I show how the latter strategically elicit the formers' participation by systematically targeting and manipulating their expressive desires.

Third, and most broadly, the purpose of the book is to suggest that the methodologically driven division of the social sciences—very crudely, into the legacies of Karl Marx, Max Weber, Emile Durkheim, and Sigmund Freud on the one hand, and Adam Smith, Kenneth Arrow, Anthony Downs, and Mancur Olson on the other—forecloses many types of understandings of political behaviors that would otherwise be at our disposal. The latter trend in social science, captured today in rational, public, and social choice theory, has taught us to seek out individuals' incentive-driven behavior and provided the methods to aggregate such behavior in order to determine how groups will behave. The same schools, however, by necessity also have remained explicitly agnostic about the origin of preferences, about what determines the underlying individual-level incentives in the first place. These approaches for the most part have also been unsuccessful in approaching instances where the value of participation emerges from an attachment to a group of fellow participants— where the value of participation is *endogenous* to participation itself. It is here that we should widen our approach by turning to the legacy of the first group. In this book I draw a theoretical microfoundation from social theory and anthropology. Analytically, I operationalize this microfoundation with simple tools drawn from microeconomics. And substantively, I provide a characterization of the mass behavior of voters and consumers whose participation, at least in part, is driven by a desire to establish, for themselves and for others, who they are.

The core thought behind this book began a very long time ago and developed through a wide variety of contexts. It is therefore both necessary and appropriate to thank a large number of people with highly diverse interests. I first thought about some of the issues in this book when writing an essay on the role of identity in the modern German literature of Max Frisch. Frisch's ideas revolve around the problematic interplay between an individual, his identity, and his surrounding collective as his identity is defined (Frisch's protagonists were always male). This literature convinced me that I wanted to be a social scientist. I had been introduced to it by Anne Gray. She encouraged me to pursue that ambition, so it is appropriate that I thank her first. It reveals her influence that many of the ideas in that first attempt at a research project should have found their way into this book fifteen years later.

As an undergraduate in anthropology and social theory at Cambridge University, I began the best three years of my life. Among my teachers and supervisors, Ernest Gellner, Keith Hart, and Graham McCann all had very different ideas as to what it meant to be a social scientist. Like everyone else there, they pushed me very hard and consistently disapproved of everything I did. To the disapproval of two, one supervised me on a research project on celebrity and interpretive social theory, which was my introduction to Continental twentieth-century social thought in the context of (what in this book I think of as "expressive") mass behavior. It is again very striking to recognize the extent to which all three continue to matter in the very different work I do now.

During my first two years as a graduate student in political economy and government at Harvard, I changed my focus from the "classical" continental-European definition of political economy to its American, neoclassical-economic one. After taking a course with Thomas Schelling, I wrote a paper that became a first outline of what eventually would be my doctoral dissertation. Schelling encouraged me to pursue the topic and, characteristic of his advice, to keep it as simple and transparent as possible. He saw the project twice more— once when it was a completed doctoral dissertation, and once when it had just become a book manuscript. Michael O'Hare and Joe Kalt were supportive of the project very early on, despite the painfully crude stage it was in.

At the Harvard Government Department Kenneth Shepsle climbed on board the dissertation in its final year and a half and quickly became the chair of my committee. He has remained an advisor of all kinds ever since. Gary King's enthusiasm for all things researchable mattered greatly, and the Harvard-MIT Research Training Group (RTG) in Positive Political Economy, under Jim Alt's direction, provided not only much-needed National Science Foundation funding, but even more needed (and appreciated) training. My former fellow graduate students Lisa Davis, Janet Gornick, and Francois Degeorge remain important friends to this day, as does Karl Kronebusch, whose ongoing thinking about the argument has not only brought to light many very useful sources, but has also been very flattering. I spent many hours with Prasannan Parthasarathi discussing this topic in the context of economic history and social theory. Mohan Penubarti, whom I met in my last year as a graduate student, while both of us were Fellows at the Harvard Data Center, continues to be a much treasured friend, as well as my coauthor in various projects on statistical methodology. It is a special pleasure, after all these years, finally to be able to thank Molly Brodie properly. Molly read many original chapter drafts several times. Her generous friendship, together with her ability to blend criticism, encouragement, and advice shaped this book in many different ways.

I was fortunate to begin my academic career at NYU's Department of Politics and in fabulous New York City. Russell Hardin's enthusiasm from the moment I arrived was as flattering as his willingness to supply continuously what he once called "grist" for my "expressive mill." Youssef Cohen's friendship became evident the day he remarked, that "only a nut" would refer to a jukebox in order to understand the equivalency between presidential candidates and soft drinks. Similarly important (though much more nicely put) encouragement came from Steven Brams—who was welcoming from the very first time I visited the department—and from George Downs—who has been encouraging even before joining the department as chair. I learn from Michael Gilligan almost every day, and did even more so when together we taught a graduate course on positive political economy. With Stathis Kalyvas I have spent a great many hours discussing the ideas of this book, as well as the social sciences more generally. This time has been enjoyable, particularly because much of it was spent in Japanese restaurants. Mark Lilla, who leaves for Chicago as I write this, provided valuable comments on the first four chapters of this book.

I also thank Farhad Kazemi, Bernard Manin, Pasquale Pasquino, Marek Kaminsky, Jeff Silver, Libby Wood, Anna Harvey, Tim Mitchell, Mark Roelofs, and Bertell Ollman, all of whom have contributed to this book with their criticisms and ideas. Amanda Friedenberg, Heidi Galli, Sona Nadenichek, and Bill Pink all provided research assistance at different times. I am especially grateful to Heidi.

Parts of this book have been presented or discussed at various political science and economics meetings, at several conferences under the generous sponsorship of the Liberty Fund, as well as at the University of Chicago, and the Harvard Business School. I am grateful to Kathy Bawn, Tyler Cowen, Mark Hansen, Mel Hinich, Jonathan Krasno, David Laitin, Jan Leighley, Bill Mitchell, Barry O'Neill and Randy Simmons for their ideas and criticisms. I remember with particular gratitude a walk with Michael Munger through Pasadena, discussing an early draft he had read. I came to know Susan Herbst through this work, after sending her a paper on expressive voting, and she quickly and enthusiastically responded with many important suggestions, as well as with the request to see the book manuscript. My communications with Samuel Popkin also began only after he had seen the manuscript. He, too, was exceedingly generous with his encouragement and volunteered many valuable suggestions.

Susan Perrin read an earlier version of the entire manuscript while sharing my dismay when split infinitives became "legal." It is customary to note that any of a manuscript's remaining errors are the fault of the author's. In this case I would like to note that any remaining split infinitives are Susan's fault. Malcolm Litchfield and Chuck Myers at Princeton University Press must be the most patient people I have met. They won't believe me when they read this, but I promise not to try their patience like this again.

It is a great pleasure to thank friends who have played a large role in the book, without necessarily having had much direct contact with it. I knew of, and much admired, Michael Gilsenan's work while I was still an undergraduate at Cambridge and he was at Oxford. Now that we have met and are both at NYU, we have become close friends, for which I am most deeply grateful. I barely knew Ben Hunt while we overlapped in graduate school, got to know him well while we were colleagues at NYU, and now consider him a very important friend. I have also become very close to Kevin van Duuglas-Ittu and Dabney McKinley. To distort a Weberian distinction, their "professions" are to make what are considered the best martinis in Manhattan, whereas their "vocations" are to explore their knowledge of literature and psychoanalytic thought in their own writings . . . only in New York! I am thankful—and certainly comfortable—to be sitting at the intersection of both callings. I first met Charles Ferguson two years ago and am blessed to be calling him a friend. Bob Jackson's friendship, and that of Vic Fontaine, Larry Kaye, John Caskey, and Paul Coogan have left a strong imprint on the first half of this book.

Finally, if Anne Gray originally opened the door and indicated a way to social thought, Hilary Beattie has begun to show where one could still go. As a consequence this book has come to seem like a preliminary thought along the way, rather than a conclusion. Tyler Perrin will be as pleased as I am that this book is done. I owe much to her calm confidence, loving support, patience, and ability to be kind to a crazed person finishing a book. And, at last, I thank my parents. We never discussed any of the ideas in this book, and yet they determined them greatly. This book is dedicated to them, with all my gratitude for many things.

A LOGIC OF EXPRESSIVE CHOICE

Chapter One

EXPRESSIVE CHOICE AND MASS PARTICIPATION

DURING HIS closing statements to the third and final televised debate of the 1992 presidential election campaign, incumbent candidate George Bush faced the national audience and told prospective voters that his electoral victory was certain. A few moments later, Bush again emphasized the overwhelming popularity of his candidacy, but added that he would be incapable of winning unless voters chose to participate in the election. The two statements are seemingly in contradiction, for though the first stresses an impossibility of defeat, the second requests assistance in securing victory. As I will argue in this chapter and explore in the remainder of this book, George Bush's first remark targeted the "symbolic" or "expressive" component of prospective participants' motivation, whereas the second focused on the "instrumental" or "outcome-oriented" component of that motivation. The fact that the two claims combined involve the use of contradictory signals in the space of only a few sentences reflects why the practice of modern campaigning by many has come to be considered an art form.

In this book I seek to understand various forms of mass participation—including voters' participation in elections, citizens' participation in interest groups, and consumers' participation in the market—as instances wherein participants are at least in part motivated by expressive concerns. As I will explore, in all these realms individuals often are motivated by a desire to express their tastes, or preferences, because such expression has direct influence on who they are—on their identity. For example, and most simply, it is the voter's statement of her preference for the Democratic candidate, through voting, that *makes* the voter a Democrat. This self-definition through voting will at least in part determine her motivation to support a candidate. Following the very same logic, candidates' campaigns are designed to draw voters into an election by making it attractive for them to identify with their vote choice. Consequently, to understand voting fully requires us not merely to map out the instrumental consequence of the individual's vote on the electoral result, as in modern political economy we most typically do; it additionally requires us to investigate the expressive, or in some sense *existential*, consequence of the vote for the voter herself. The purpose of this book is to do precisely this: to define, identify, and explore a system, or economy, of expressive incentives. This economy is one wherein participants are driven by expressive or symbolic concerns and wherein producers—be they campaign managers, interest-group leaders, or industrial producers and their advertisers—elicit participation by strategically manipulating these concerns. In other words, *the purpose of this book is to propose, define, and explore a logic of expressive choice.*

To approach political participation in economic or incentive-driven terms is, of course, not new, even though existing attempts do not assume an expressive microfoundation. Instead, economic approaches typically are couched in instrumental or (electoral-) outcome-related terms. These approaches date back more than forty years to the publication of Downs's *An Economic Theory of Democracy* (1957) and continue to develop in rational choice theory. It is ironic, however, that although large-scale electoral behavior has been the intellectual origin for rational choice theory, this area is also where it has been least successful.

Most significantly, it is here that it has suffered the collective action problem. Olson's *Logic of Collective Action* (1965) originally was intended as an explanation for why collectives did not mobilize to provide public goods, and this explanation was based on the notion that in the production of public goods, individuals face a dominant incentive to free-ride. Olson's original focus was on interest groups, but the argument quickly was extended to elections and to other forms of political participation. Ironically, shortly after Olson's work was published, a "participation explosion" was witnessed in much of the Western world. As Hirschman notes (1971b, 5), "astoundingly large numbers of citizens, far from attempting to get a free ride, have been taking to the streets, to the nation's capital, or to other places where they expect to exert some influence for change. In this connection, it is interesting to note that while economists keep worrying about the free rider problem, political scientists have become increasingly concerned about the 'paradox of participation.'" What began as a methodological explanation for political inactivity quickly turned into a methodologically driven puzzle questioning why political participation should be as high as it was. A significant part of the political science literature since the mid-1960s, subsequently, has been concerned with providing a response to this question. The centrality of the question—and the difficulty associated with it—is well characterized by Fiorina, who infamously called it the "paradox that ate rational choice theory" (1990, 334).

The purpose of this book is not to "solve" the paradox of participation, but to demonstrate how the paradox itself rests on a methodological foundation of outcome orientation that is inappropriate in many instances of large-scale collective behavior. The approach I develop here is based on a fundamental assumption that individuals do not necessarily participate in collective action in order to produce outcomes, but instead often do so in order to express who they are by attaching themselves to such outcomes. As I will show, this approach leads us to predict political participation where previously we did not. The approach of this book is one that contains the detailed contours of a logic of expressively motivated choice. This logic is one that will tell us under what conditions expressive incentives are particularly high, and how candidates—like George Bush in the opening illustration of this chapter—will attempt to manipulate these expressive incentives in order to elicit prospective voters' electoral support.

1.1   APPROACHING NON-INSTRUMENTAL CHOICE

George Bush's stressing the difficulty of winning unless voters choose to participate in the election can be argued to be consistent with an instrumental Olsonian prescription. One might argue that to stress to voters the importance of participating in the election is for the candidate to exaggerate the perceived instrumental benefits of participation by ascribing to each and every individual vote an instrumental potency that lies well beyond statistical reality.[1] In the context of such instrumentalist explanation, however, Bush's expression of assured victory stands at odds with Olsonian theory: if such victory is indeed certain, why should individuals feel compelled to participate in the election still? If free-riding on others' participation poses a threat to collective action, then a candidate's explicit electoral confidence—if credible—can only further enhance that threat.

Yet such campaigning is consistent with the economy of expressive incentives proposed in this book. If the voter's motivation is one of attachment—I attach myself to a public outcome, rather than produce it—the basic collective action question will need to be recast. For example, instead of asking "Why should I face the steep cost of participation when an outcome is already being produced, regardless of my participation?" one can now recognize that "because a significant number of individuals are already producing the desired outcome, I can, *at the mere cost of participation*, purchase for myself the status of outcome-producer." In the instrumental context of production, the cost of participation is steep relative to the expected value of the out-

---

[1] The actual potency of a vote will be discussed in chapter three.

come, which is virtually indistinguishable from zero.[2] In the expressive context of attachment, in contrast, the cost is low, relative to the value of participation: in the present example, it is precisely in the event that everybody else's vote is expected to generate a Bush victory that imbues my participation with higher expected value, because I can now expect to become someone who will have gotten George Bush elected. If the logic is one of identification or attachment—of Being—rather than one of production—of Doing—then the relevant probabilities that mediate the benefits of my participation will be different.

This is one simple expressively based scenario, and many others are possible, as I will discuss. As I will also show, this particular scenario and its motivational microfoundation provide sufficient basis to the phenomenon of electoral bandwagons or momentum. Momentum in public opinion across subsequent surveys, and in elections across subsequent primaries, empirically have been modeled by political scientists with great success (e.g., Bartels 1988). As future chapters will show, political scientists have been far less successful in providing a satisfactory explanation for the existence of these bandwagons. They have not managed simultaneously to explain both (a) how *individuals* react to the behavior of others, and (b) how such individual-level reactions *aggregate* to generate collective momentum. As I review in chapter three, typically they have done either one or the other, and more commonly still, they have based their approach on a microlevel theory that is internally inconsistent. Such inconsistency is absent from the expressively based explanation offered here, and the present approach will focus both on the individual and the resultant collective level.

1.2 METHODOLOGICAL, BUT NOT ONTOLOGICAL, INDIVIDUALISM

Throughout the approach of this book and its analysis of large-scale participation, the critical focus rests not on rational choice theory, but on the instrumental microfoundations with which rational choice theorists have approached this type of large-scale action. In other words, the purpose here is not to characterize the behavior of voters and others as nonrational, or irrational. Instead, it is to approach such behavior as *noninstrumental*. Beyond this distinction, at the microlevel the approach in this book in many ways follows a rational choice

---

[2] The exact basis to that calculation will be presented in chapter two.

approach—which is why its discussion of expressive choice began there. Several reasons motivate this.

First, in rational choice theory, collectives are the analytical aggregates of individuals, which is to say that group behavior can be predicted through summing up the behavior of individuals. This, of course, is the analytic fodder of social choice theory and its more politically (and often polemically) oriented public choice cousin. Unlike for rational, social, and public choice theorists, however, the methodological individualism that drives the present approach is not derived from, or synonymous with, an ontological individualism. This is most pronounced in the role of preferences, tastes, or opinions.

For these diverse choice theorists, individuals' preferences are exogenous. They are in place before the theorist enters the scene and are put into place by powers independent of (and thus logically prior to) the social situation that is being studied. Theorists, consequently, can afford to be entirely agnostic about the origin of preferences. The present approach, in contrast, assumes that preferences to a significant extent *emerge* from social context itself: following anthropologists and social theorists, preferences, values, and beliefs all emerge from social practice. They are endogenous to the social context in that they are generated by interaction within that very context.

For example, as I will argue in this book, one's beliefs and values concerning a political candidate will be conditioned by information concerning both the candidate's standing among the remaining electorate and the identity of the candidate's other supporters—which I will call the *who* and *how many* dimensions of participation. If my motivation is expressive, then expressive significance will be determined by such context. Expressively focused campaigns, therefore, are concerned with defining, changing, and manipulating context: in that sense, George Bush's stressing of the certainty of victory is an attempt at eliciting participation by generating information about context. More specifically, it is information about what the remaining electorate intends to do that introduces information about *what it means to be* a Bush supporter. Preference for presidential candidate Bush, in this light, is generated in social context, and the purpose of electoral campaigning is to manipulate that context.

Such preference endogeneity in itself is sufficient to separate methodological from ontological individualism. As I have noted, the behavior of collectives, in my approach, can be approached methodologically as an aggregate of individuals' behavior. However, the preferences, tastes, opinions, values, and beliefs that motivate this behavior will stem from the collective. If the former—the study of collective *action*—invites a micro-to-macro approach, then the latter—the study of *preferences underlying such action*—invites a macro-to-micro approach. *Consequently, in a much broader sense than in rational choice theory we typically employ, this approach concerns itself with (social) equilibrium conditions.*

A second manner in which this study of expressive choice models itself after rational choice theory lies in its focus on a system, economy, or logic of incentives. This approach is by no means the first to suggest that voters may be driven by noninstrumental or non-outcome-oriented motivations: in chapter three I provide rough inventory of alternative motivations that rational choice theorists and their critics have put forth in response to the paradox of participation. However, the vast majority of approaches that have acknowledged the possible existence of noninstrumental motivation have either merely added a noninstrumental static term to an existent instrumentally driven model—where the noninstrumental term simply absorbs all that which the instrumental terms of the model cannot—or they have proposed a break with a formal incentive-driven approach altogether. The dominant assumption has been that if voters, consumers, activists, and other individuals are driven by expressive concerns, their actions are less systematic or predictable, or, for that matter, less "rational." As I explore in chapter four, a different rationality can be noted to exist, one much closer to what Max Weber called "substantive" or "value" rationality (*Wertrationalität*), as opposed to outcome-oriented, or what he called "formal," rationality (*Zweckrationalität*). The task of this book is to show how this different—and as I will claim, *richer*—flavor of rationality does not preclude an aggregation of microlevel incentives into a coherent macrolevel logic, or "economy" of incentives.

1.3 Overview

The first part of this book ("Theory") extends through the next three chapters and provides a theoretical and methodological framing of expressive motivation. The second part ("Analysis") extends through chapters five, six, seven, and eight and provides a historical exploration of the rise of an expressive economy, and subsequently some examples of how this economy lends itself to simple formalization. Chapter nine concludes the book.

In chapter two I sketch in outline the features of the economy of expressive motivation to be developed in this book. Particular attention will be paid to those features that distinguish this economy of expressive choice from instrumental-choice economies presented in the literature.

In chapter three I return to the collective action literature and show how internal inconsistencies have forced rational choice scholars to separate out the study of electoral *turnout* from electoral *choice*. I provide a review of the paradox of participation and of the types of responses this paradox has elicited in the literature. In chapter four I extend my methodological frame as I draw on anthropology and social theory to construct a theoretical microfoundation on the basis of which expressive motivation and expressively motivated choice can be defined and operationalized in the analysis that follows.

In chapter five I provide a comparative history of how citizens' expressive motivation has become a target for those eliciting mass participation. Specifically, I show how the rise of mass markets early in the twentieth century has required industrial producers and advertisers to switch their marketing efforts to an expressively focused approach, and how political campaigns have faced precisely the same requirement with the rise of a television-based mass media since the early 1950s. As I will show, the identical analytical requirements of eliciting participation in these two different types of mass markets has led political campaigns to invite marketing experts to refocus their efforts in eliciting electoral support.

In chapters six, seven, and eight I formalize aspects of the historical argument, as I reproduce in formal terms some of the marketing and campaign practices I identified in chapter five, on the basis of the theoretical microfoundation established in chapters two, three, and four. I embed my analysis of expressively focused campaign practices in the microlevel theory of expressive voting and consumption explored in the first part of the book. As will become evident, the approach of this book allows us to go much beyond noting that citizens do participate where previously we expected them not to. Specifically, we can identify conditions under which electoral (or, for that matter, market) support is stable, and we can identify the consequences on such stability of producer strategies like negative campaigning. Similarly, I will show how instrumentally focused campaign strategies in fact reduce for voters the expressive value of participation, and why electoral campaigns therefore are always better off including in their large-scale campaigns an expressive focus. Throughout the formal approach, I will place great emphasis on the robustness of the analysis: to be sure, it would be of little value to propose a model that works only if all voters are expressively motivated, and if all these voters are expressively motivated in exactly the same way. As I will demonstrate, the predictions I draw initially in the context of a stylized economy in which *all* participants are assumed to be motivated expressively will still hold in the context of an economy where only *some* participants are. Finally, in the closing chapter I summarize the conclusions generated by this theory and discuss some normative implications.

I now begin with a sketch of an economy of expressive choice and mass participation. For the sake of simplicity and efficiency in illustration, and in order to break with the terms typically associated with the study of electoral behavior, I draw this outline not in voting, but in what I will call "jukebox" participation. I subsequently relate the identified features to the electoral realm in order to motivate the analytical focus of the chapters that follow.

PART ONE

THEORY

Chapter Two

A JUKEBOX MODEL OF PARTICIPATION

> It's Sinatra's world—we just live in it.
> *(Lapel button from the 1950s)*

BOSTON'S NORTH END is an area best known for its residential and culinary charm. Thirty-odd, mostly Italian, restaurants and cafés grace its neighborhood, as do several food and kitchen stores. Among its establishments, one café stands out as a favorite venue of the crowds. Caffe Vittoria is famous for its cappuccino, its cannoli, and its Sambuca—its "caps, cans, and sams." It is equally famous, perhaps, for constantly being crowded, for its spirited decor—including a copper-colored ceiling and a painted mural of a southern-Italian coastline—for its impolite wait staff, and—most significantly to us—for its constantly blaring jukebox.

Patrons wishing to hear a musical selection feed the jukebox with a sum of money for which they get to enter their wish. Since most of the time the machine is already playing others' selections, participating customers typically need to wait their turn before they get to hear their choice. What is interesting is that the individual customer's payment may not be responsible for the jukebox's rendition of his or her selection. There are several aspects to the nature of participation in the jukebox arena that separate the customer's contribution from the jukebox outcome.

First, the jukebox does not reveal which requests have already been made and, therefore, what songs are already queued for public consumption. An individual stepping up to the machine may well be choosing a selection that would have been played in the absence of his or her own participation, due to someone else's prior request of the same selection. It is unlikely, however, that participants will ever become aware of this redundancy of their participation, for a second jukebox characteristic is that the machine plays a selection only once, regardless of how often it is requested, or, more significantly, how often it is paid for. For example, a duplicate request of Frank Sinatra's "New York, New York," a Caffe Vittoria favorite, will produce only one rendition of the song. Consequently, rather than permit customers to regret the redundancy of their participation, the machine allows each participant to lay claim on having produced the "New

York, New York" outcome in the café. Participants are capable of doing so only, of course, if they do not directly witness each other's choices—a condition enhanced by the jukebox's third characteristic, which contributes to the shielding of individuals from the selections of their fellow participants. Not only is participation inherently private, in that I witness my neighbor's stepping to the jukebox but do not see what selection it is that he or she is making; additionally, the jukebox also *shields* me from the identity of other participants in that it does not play musical selections in the order in which they were made. Observers, consequently, are not able to attribute specific jukebox selections to specific participants by mapping the observed sequence of participation onto the sequence of selections played. Therefore, if the difficulty of identifying specific song requestors is already a somewhat likely consequence of the first two jukebox characteristics, it becomes a near-certain consequence of the third characteristic, the jukebox's scrambling of requested renditions.

It is at this point in a decision setting that we expect political economists and decision theorists to infer, postulate, or attempt to measure individuals' utility derived from participation or consumption by pitting probabilities of product supply (how likely it is that the jukebox will supply the product anyway) against the cost of participation (fifty cents per request) and frame it in a context of information (the individual consumer's prior estimates of the likelihood of his or her desired product already being supplied). Standard responses to explaining phenomena such as the existence of multiple payments, where one alone would have supplied the product, are generally couched in terms of informational uncertainty.[1] Due to the jukebox's shielding mechanism, a customer simply may not know which selections are currently popular and are therefore more likely already to have been requested. Given the informational asymmetry—the jukebox knows a great deal more about the current market than do its participants—we would expect to find the producer's advantage there.

And yet such an approach appears misplaced in the current context. Rather than utilize the lack of certainty on the potential consumer's part, a fourth characteristic of the jukebox is that its manufacturer in fact *reduces* the degree of uncertainty by installing a display that constantly shows the most popular selection of the day. At the time of writing, that selection was in fact Frank Sinatra's "New York,

---

[1] In game-theoretic terms, the present uncertainty is one of incomplete information, which is one whereby "nature moves first and is unobserved by at least one of the players" (Rasmusen 1989, 53).

New York," which is relevant only in that the jukebox has been show-ing "New York, New York" to be one of the top two selections for years on end (the Italian hit "Volare" being the other). The jukebox, rather than obscure current popularity in order to elicit multiple pay-ments for a single product, on the contrary *emphasizes* current popu-larity, presumably in order to elicit multiple payments for a single product. In other words, rather than withhold from the potential con-sumer information about what is likely to be supplied anyway, the jukebox instead reveals what selections already bear a greater likeli-hood of being played, although the machine stops short of stating precisely what existing selections are. The consistency with which "New York, New York" and "Volare" share the top spot suggests that the signal of popularity *elicits* rather than dissuades individuals' con-tinued contributions: in the terms of economists and game theorists, "New York, New York" and "Volare" appear to be stable equilibrium outcomes in the decision framework.[2]

A preliminary conclusion to be drawn at this point is that, at a minimum, consumers are in part motivated by something other than a concern with outcome. If in fact the Frank Sinatra outcome were all the typical participant cared about, the revenue-focused jukebox man-ufacturer would be foolish to signal the greater redundancy of partici-pating in a particular selection, thereby reducing the probability of receiving multiple payments for a single request. More important, we have seen that indicating the song's popularity does not appear to destabilize the stable-equilibrium nature of the Sinatra outcome. What is it, then, if not outcome-oriented, or instrumentally rational, motiva-tion that drives the participant? Stated differently, what is it that the manufacturer of jukeboxes, *who is also the manufacturer or producer of participation in the café's jukebox arena*, taps into through the installation of the popular-song display, as well as through the three other jukebox characteristics previously noted?

I argue that participants in settings such as the jukebox arena are at least in part motivated by *expressive* concerns. Participation is not only a means for me to create the Frank Sinatra outcome on the jukebox—it is also a way for me to establish, reaffirm, demonstrate, and express my Frank Sinatra*ness* to the rest of the world, as well as to myself. Knowing the song's popularity among the café's patrons will have a very direct effect on the expressive value I attach to my own partici-pation. In this sense, my motivation to participate is grounded not in the calculative realm of strategically producing states of the world, but in the interpretive realm of *attaching* myself to those states. In

---

[2] The nature of these equilibria will be explored more precisely in chapter six.

other words, what matters is not so much my actual instrumental contribution to the collective outcome, but my ability to claim to others, as well as to myself, to have been responsible for the outcome.[3] As I previewed in the Introduction and will argue with greater precision in the next chapter, participants are motivated not only by desires of "Doing," but also by desires of "Being," whereby the latter refers to an identity dimension that signifies an individual's attachment to Frank Sinatra. Participation—performing X—in this context is not motivated by creating or "doing" Y, but by the desire of "being" an X-performer: there is a *consumption benefit* to performing X (Brennan and Buchanan 1984; Uhlaner 1989; Schuessler 2000).

Several of the noted jukebox features should already resonate with some of the questions raised in the Introduction with respect to electoral behavior. I now explore the jukebox logic of participation by turning back to the wider sphere of mass participation in both electoral and industrial market settings. I begin by identifying the relevant features.

2.1 CLAIMING POPULARITY

In the context of the jukebox I asked why it was that the jukebox manufacturer announced the popularity of particular selections, if that also indicated a likely redundancy of participation. I already asked a corresponding question in the mass-electoral context: why do presidential and other large-scale electoral candidates indicate to prospective voters, in the days leading up to the election, that they are already winning, if this is likely to indicate a redundancy of electoral participation?[4] Polls published by candidates systematically deviate, in their respective favor, from polls published by independent pollsters (Bartels 1988; Cantril 1991; Edelman 1988; Herbst 1993; Popkin 1991). Yet, as I have noted, if participation indeed were instrumentally motivated, any persuasion that my favored candidate is already being elected further should dissuade me from facing the cost of partaking in the election also: I should simply free-ride on others' efforts.[5] Here, as before, one might conclude that participation is motivated at least

[3] Note that the *idiom* is still an instrumental one, as the claim is about determining an outcome. However, the *mechanism*, as I will argue, is one of expressive attachment.

[4] "Redundancy" here is defined as the extent of participation beyond that necessary to ensure a candidate's electoral victory. The analysis of the coming chapters remains fundamentally unchanged if we include other candidate concerns. These may include the goal of winning by a landslide, rather than just securing victory, and so forth.

[5] The exact nature of this free-riding, as well as alternative motivational impediments such as "cheap rides" and the like, will be reviewed in greater detail in the next chapter.

in part by something other than concern over outcome. Both here and in the jukebox scenario, the prospective participant is provided by the producer with information indicating that the outcome is already likely to be had, regardless of his or her own participation.

If participant motivation is not instrumentally rational, outcome-oriented, or rooted in the domain of Doing, then again it should be considered grounded in the expressive domain of Being. Rather than viewing individuals' participation in elections as means to selecting their favored (assume Democratic) candidates, we might additionally view participation as individuals' expression of their "Democratness," or of their *becoming* Democrats. Once again, in addition to strategic concerns of creating a preferred outcome, participation is a means of attaching oneself to an outcome. And, once again, we might posit a consumption benefit, though it now needs to be shown how, unlike in the case of its instrumental counterpart, this consumption benefit may typically thrive in instances where producers successfully persuade prospective participants that their candidate is already winning.

Instrumentally, we have seen that such settings are less conducive to participation, as the implicit redundancy of participation raises the dominant incentive to free-ride. Yet the instrumental incentive to free-ride loses all relevance in the expressive context, for the consumption benefit of participation is not one that others can free-ride on: to *be* Democrat, one must participate in voting for the Democratic candidate (or at least, to others and to oneself, lie about having voted for that candidate in the election). Because the value of participation emerges not from its outcome but from the process of participation itself, free-riding is no longer possible. In economic terms, whereas outcomes or states of the world are "public goods," expressive or symbolic returns to participation are "private goods."

Finally, we should note that producers' claims concerning the greater public support for their products (be they candidates, political causes, or physical goods) extend well beyond electoral politics. Interest groups seeking to sell memberships stress the vast support of a particular cause among the public. Private industrial producers, by stressing through advertising that their product is more widely liked than that of their competitors, routinely invite prospective consumers to partake in consumption (e.g., Magiero 1993). Simulated taste and other preference tests are frequently employed in beverage and car commercials alike, and here, as before, individuals' participation is elicited through some (often quite abstract) confrontation with the majority preferences of the masses.[6] As I now turn to investigate—

---

[6] Two points should be made here. First, as is central to social choice theory, the very

and as I discussed in the context of the original jukebox scenario in shielding terms—individuals in these instances are confronted with the masses not through recognizing whom, exactly, these masses consist of, but by perceiving them simply anonymously to exist.

2.2   HORIZONTAL SHIELDING OF FELLOW PARTICIPANTS

A second jukebox feature found in the context of presidential and other large-scale political campaigns is the frequent shielding of fellow voters from one another. In the original context of the jukebox, the machine's strong emphasis of a selection's popularity (its popular-song display) is complemented by a shielding mechanism of who else prefers a particular selection (its scrambled sequence), which prevents individuals from mapping the sequence of selections played onto the observed sequence of participation. This, coupled with the jukebox's acceptance of multiple payments for a single product (or single rendition), has various consequences. First, though I witness a neighboring customer's stepping to the jukebox, making payment, and entering some selection, I do not know which song he or she has chosen, despite the fact that we both simultaneously consume it. Consumption, in standard terms, is public (purchaser and nonpurchaser alike partake in it); participation in bringing about the product is semipublic: I witness my neighbor's participation, though I do not know what it is he or she has selected. In addition to those two dimensions, however, consumption is also emphatically private. For when I return from my own trip to the machine and, minutes later, hear my selection "New York, New York," it is more than likely—given the selection's popularity—that several other individuals in the establishment will, much like myself, proudly tell their table friends that they were the producers of that selection. Due to the shielding mechanisms in place, several individuals are able simultaneously to attach themselves to

---

term "majority preferences" in a collective setting is problematic. I use it here with little hesitation as, indeed, what is relevant in the current context is an abstract confrontation of the participant with some alleged preferences of a collective. Hence, even if the term is analytically contentious, its use as a signal to induce participation is sufficiently real because its perception is what is relevant. Second, information economists (and others) typically argue that there is an instrumental component to a majority's preferences, either in that it is a cheap source of information concerning a good's quality, or in that there may be some "network" component to a good's properties (its use to the individual depends on how many others are using the same standard). Chapters three and four will indicate the difference between such approaches and those, such as the one I present here, that are interested in the noninstrumental, or expressive, component of participant motivation, and how these will be affected by majority practices.

the product by claiming to have created it. Even if we are all aware that our personal participation, strictly, may have been redundant, the natural shielding in place will permit us to view the Sinatra rendition as an opportunity better to demonstrate to ourselves and to others our Sinatraness: we all attached ourselves to the product by paying for it, and at the very least, our participation would have been sufficient to create the outcome.

The strict shielding requirement falls away in the electoral context, because an electoral result is not one that can be brought about by a single individual to begin with. In the jukebox case, my not knowing for certain whether the preferred song would already have been chosen may enhance my ability to attach myself to the outcome, for I can now claim single-handedly to have brought it about. The very essence of electoral decision making, in contrast, is explicitly collective. What the two settings do share, however, is that in both the electoral and the jukebox contexts, I attach myself to some abstractly defined collective of Sinatra customers and Democrats, respectively. In both cases, I will not know or observe the vast majority of my fellow participants firsthand. My self-ascription as Democrat or Sinatra consumer, consequently, consists of an abstract attachment to a largely anonymous crowd. In the electoral context, too, this is aided by a natural shielding in place, though, as I now preview and will soon explore in greater detail, campaigning may strategically strengthen such shielding.

Indeed, producers in both the electoral and market contexts, rely on and enhance this horizontal anonymity. Although political candidates consistently emphasize the majority's support, they do not always emphasize who it is, precisely, that offers such support. Candidates frequently reject endorsements in that they assume any identification with a specific type of voter will dissuade other potential voters' participation. In 1988, for example, Jesse Jackson rejected endorsement of gay rights groups, whereas George Bush's campaign went to great lengths in 1992 to obfuscate any form of endorsement by the National Rifle Association.

In the consumer market context, for example, recording companies spend vast resources on securing their product's top placing on the best-seller list, the "Billboard Charts" (Dannen 1990), while at the same time going to great lengths to undermine fan clubs.[7] Why? Fan clubs, surely, are the ultimate consumption institution, built entirely around a product, and should therefore aid product sales. Yet fan

[7] David Currie, editor of *Starzone: The Official David Bowie Magazine*, in conversation, Watford, UK, July 31, 1986.

clubs are also arenas in which consumers actively witness fellow participants' consumption. As I will show in chapters five and six—for reasons of different participants attaching different interpretive features to one and the same good—the utility derived by the average consumer from consumption is likely to diminish as consumption truly becomes a joint activity.

Advertisers of industrial mass products consistently emphasize their lead in sales, but rarely reveal the identity characteristics of fellow consumers. Research in marketing has in fact shown that even the use of a celebrity consumer as spokesperson in product advertisement is considerably less effective in raising overall product sales, when compared to the use of a fictional spokesperson about whom the potential consumer knows nothing (Gail 1992; Walker 1992). Rather than focus on the specific identity characteristics of fellow consumers, mass advertisements replace demographic-specific messages with vague, all-encompassing references: to note one well-known example, there simply are no specific identity characteristics associated with "the Pepsi Generation."[8] The Coca-Cola company, in recent years, has given up on portraying human consumers altogether, turning instead to the use of animated polar bears. As with political candidates, as well as with recording celebrities, any confrontation with *who* it is, exactly, that consumes a particular beverage may well elicit additional consumption by some, but also deter the participation of other potential consumers. Beyond a level of existing participation, when the heterogeneity of prospective consumers exceeds a threshold level, confrontation with fellow participants will begin to result in a net decline in participation levels. The importance of shielding participants from their fellows is derived from the fact that expressively motivated consumption is a function not of exogenous taste (how the product appeals to me in blind taste tests), but of interpretive, or "semiotic," considerations (what it means to me to be consuming the product). If such meaning varies with the perceived identity characteristics of fellow participants, then it may be in the producer's interest, beyond a certain level of aggregate participation, to shield the potential participant from those characteristics, as they will become a liability.

And, finally, producers' attempts at shielding consumers from fellow participants occurs not only in true mass markets, but at times also in settings similar in scale to that of our Italian café and its jukebox. Movie theaters, through their arrangement of entrance and

---

[8] As I will discuss in my historical account of chapter five, the "Pepsi Generation" campaign entered the Cola wars in the 1960s (Tedlow 1990).

seating, and their use of low lighting before and after the show, prevent us from interacting with fellow moviegoers other than by perceiving their silhouettes or hearing their collective laugh. Similarly, many restaurants elicit our consumption by stressing their popularity ("everyone" eats here), although once we participate, interaction with other customers is curtailed, as we are usually placed in that great American restaurant institution: the booth.

2.3   HORIZONTAL SHIELDING OF COMPETING PRODUCERS

The jukebox scenario represents a peculiar example of an arena of participation characterized by the presence of a single producer of participation. In the jukebox's attempt at eliciting contributions from the café's patrons, in the event of failure, potential participants will abstain from participating. In contrast, the electoral setting and the mass market setting are both characterized by the presence of (multiple) competing producers. Republican campaign managers will want to attract potential voters away from both a state of inactivity and the Democratic opponent. Industrial producers seek for their customers not only among nonconsumers, but also among consumers of competing products. In both instances, producers are concerned both with the volume of aggregate participation in their good and with their good's market share. We should therefore step beyond the single-producer scope of the jukebox and explore how competing producers of participation are likely to interact strategically.

In the previous characterization of the shielding of fellow participants, I inferred that if participation is in part motivated by an interpretive, or meaning-based, consumption benefit, then firsthand observation of others' participation will reduce the interpretive scope of what it means to the prospective participant to vote Democrat or to choose Sinatra. If Sinatra were known to be the characteristic choice of drunken hoodlums, the likelihood of my own partaking in Sinatra would be lower (unless, of course, I too by choice, and happily, were a drunken hoodlum). If drunken hoodlums partake in Sinatra, but I never get to see them (or, in the café, I see them but do not know that it was they who made the jukebox selection), my nonhoodlum Sinatra disposition would remain intact.

An interesting equivalent observation can be made with respect to competing producers' (rather than participants') shielding from one another. As I will argue with reference to the strategic use of political ambiguity, political candidates frequently choose not to take stands on their opponents. If the candidate's aim is to elicit a multiplicity of interpretive inducements among a variety of prospective participants, then he or she would limit the interpretive breadth of electoral appeal by taking specific issue with opponents. A functional equivalent in the industrial context of mass production is that, with the exception of few consumer items—notably, computer products, automobiles, and long-distance telephone services (Jaben 1992)—direct-comparison ads that take concrete issue with the characteristics of opposing brands are fairly rare (Boddewyn and Marton 1978). In recent consumer-marketing research, they in fact have been shown to be relatively less effective when compared to self-focused merit ads (Jaben 1992). In both cases, therefore, we would expect producers to abstain from taking issue specifically with one another.

Yet what is expected and observed in the industrial context is not observed to the same extent in the domain of electoral competition. Large-scale elections in recent history have come to be observed and characterized as a series of bitter battles involving increasingly aggressive negative campaigning (Ansolabehere and Iyengar 1995; Jamieson 1992, 1996). Two reasons can be said to be responsible for this difference between the electoral and market realm. First, electoral competition occurs in a fixed time horizon, finite repeat-play context, whereas industrial competitors essentially engage in an infinite-play game. Second, whereas both industrial and electoral campaign producers aim for market share and volume, in the electoral case all strategic considerations ultimately become secondary to concerns over vote *share*, as this is both the necessary and sufficient condition to electoral victory.[9] In both the electoral and the industrial context, therefore, we do observe producer shielding, though in both contexts there will be conditions under which opponent-focused negative campaigning will occur. Negative advertising or campaigning will be expected in instances where there are a small number of competing producers and the demand for the class of good is highly inelastic: for example, long-distance telephone companies are most likely to engage in negative advertising if a very small number of them divide the market in a population that has no choice but to choose one of

[9] I employ the term "ultimately" because campaign producers' concerns over vote share are still strong, even if an electoral loss is likely. Goldenberg, in her study of 1976 congressional campaigning, reveals that competing in future elections is among candidates' concerns, and hence a high vote share is important in that it secures greater recognition in future bids (Goldenberg and Traugott 1984). Finally, even for winning candidates there will be a trade-off between vote share and vote volume: a 51 percent share of an 80 percent participating electorate's votes is lower in absolute terms than is a 60 percent share of a 40 percent participating electorate's votes. It is not unambiguously clear which victory is preferable to the candidate.

them. In instances where turnout is likely to be reduced by negative advertising—as is the case of electoral negative campaigning—trailing candidates are more likely to engage in it.

2.4 Imposing a Cost of Participation

I began by noting that participation in the jukebox café cost the participant fifty cents per song request and then proceeded to investigate how participating individuals faced participation-specific incentives that outweighed that cost. In the wider participation literature, the paradox of participation is based on the same assumption that participation involves a cost, though its focus rests on those "paradoxical" instances in which the individual participant's private costs will be greater than the private instrumental benefits derived from participation. Noting that people do, all the same, participate in large-scale collective settings wherein we would expect abstention and free-riding has led some theorists to redefine the cost of participation as a benefit (e.g., Hirschman 1971a). Attempts at seeking out the source for such benefit, however, as the next two chapters indicate, are still in their infant stages. I now explore, first, how people are in fact willing to face a participatory cost, and, second, how this cost may itself determine the magnitude of participation benefits.

Producers, both of political campaigns and of mass-consumed products, do engage in practices designed to lessen the cost of participation: this may take the form of somehow facilitating voters' access to the polling booth in the electoral context, or of the competitive pricing of goods in the industrial market context. More indirectly, it may involve electoral campaigns exaggerating the opportunity cost of abstention. I discuss the effectiveness of these different cost-focused strategies in chapter seven. At this point, however, we should note only the astounding presence, sometimes, of participants' willingness to face a cost of participation. The starkest examples are to be found not in an electorate's overcoming a cost of participation in large elections and the like because far too many levels exist for us confidently to disentangle costs and incentives there. Instead, we should look at more extreme instances of individuals facing, perhaps even *seeking out*, a participation cost such as in the case of "1-900 polling."

For example, talk show host Joan Rivers, in January 1992, asked her home viewers whether she had been too cruel in her overweight jokes targeted at TV actress Delta Burke. Viewers could record their opinion on the question by dialing one of two automated phone lines as often as they wished. Each call would represent one "vote" in the count of "public opinion," and aggregate results would be announced the following week. Most significantly, in addition to the effort of placing the call, each "vote" would cost the participant just under three dollars. Why would individuals care to contribute their participation?

Starker and more puzzling examples exist. Enterprising companies offer to the public the choice of phoning in "votes" on anything ranging from participants' favorite musicians to their preferred winners of the year's television Emmy Awards (*TV Guide*, September 4–10, 1993, Boston Edition, 220). At the stated average price of $8.25 ("$2.75 per minute, average 3 minutes"), participants are invited to phone in their preferences anonymously. As with the previous example, anonymity precludes any hope for the private return of personal fame, and the steep price of participation goes counter to any concern over personal fortune. Furthermore, the combination of participation being self-selective, together with the company's invitation to "register your choices as often as you wish," undermines any pretense that the result of the poll is of any significance beyond indicating which Emmy nominee has the fans with the greatest aggregate willingness to pay for their adoration. Most significantly, there is no statement that the results of the poll will be published or in any way used: in other words, *there is no outcome!* In the standard terms of incentives, the remarkable lack of any private instrumental returns to participation, together with the imposition of a very real cost of participation, makes this scenario a stark instance of the participation paradox. Electoral participation, therefore, is by no means the only—or for that matter a particularly dramatic—instance of the "participation paradox." What it shares with the two examples noted here is that, in instrumental terms, individuals participate in spite of a massively high ratio of private costs to private outcome-related benefits.

The present sketch of the characteristics of jukeboxlike mass participation shares with existing instrumental approaches the assumption that the magnitude of costs and benefits are independent. The costs of participating in the jukebox café, simply, was fifty cents per song request, and the outcome-determined benefit would somehow be discounted by the risk of an instrumental redundancy of participation. The costs of electoral participation can be defined in terms of the efforts associated with participating, and, again, the implication, both here and in the existing literature, has been that an expressive benefit to participation would need to overcome that cost.[10] An important

---

[10] Disutility of effort is in fact only one dimension that defines costs. In the electoral participation literature, as shown in the next chapter, the definition of "cost" has been

concern at this point addresses whether, indeed, the magnitudes of costs and returns are independent, as well as if the model to be developed in subsequent chapters will be robust to a nonindependent relationship, should the employment of such be appropriate.

Sidney Verba tells the story of near-legendary John L. Bonaccorso, a Boston resident who has been attending the Boston Pops Fourth of July Waterfront Concert for over a decade.[11] What makes Bonaccorso's achievement so spectacular, and Bonaccorso himself a celebrity, is his ability to secure a front-row seat at the exceptionally popular event every single year. At the great cost of pitching a tent at the concert site one week in advance, he beats the crowds. Several years ago, event organizers decided to reward Bonaccorso's long-standing achievement by offering to reserve for him a front-row seat, thus saving him the cost of waiting (and themselves the aggravation of dealing with an unauthorized camper). To their surprise, Bonaccorso expressed rage at the offer, noting that he had no desire to forgo the attainment efforts that traditionally preceded his attending the concert: "I'll be there through the rain, the mud, the drunks" (*New York Times*, July 2, 1987). The enjoyment of the event, apparently, was heightened by the great lengths to which Bonaccorso typically had to go to secure a good seat. His participatory enjoyment was now threatened by the producer's offering to reduce that very cost of participation: "If there's no price, there's no value," he notes. "I don't want the front unless I earn it."

The story mirrors a trend of recent participation literature that, much like the present approach, seeks to identify and classify the motivational components of participation along noninstrumental lines. Although political scientists are familiar with evidence that adverse weather conditions may suppress voter turnout in elections, they also carry at least an informal familiarity with voters proudly expressing in retrospect the great lengths to which they had to go in order to participate in an election. What the wider literature on noninstrumental benefits shares is some notion of "psychic" benefit acquired from participation itself, regardless of what the precise definition of that benefit may be. As the example of John Bonaccorso reveals, noninstrumental returns may not only follow a different pattern from instrumental returns, but in fact be *negatively correlated*: it is precisely

---

somewhat more sophisticated in that it includes not only these first-effect costs, but also considerations of opportunity costs. As my discussion of Ferejohn and Fiorina (1974) will show, the former invites the analytical tools of probabilistic cost-benefit analysis, whereas the latter calls for the application of "regret"strategems. See chapter three.

[11] In conversation, April 1994.

because instrumental incentives are stacked against him that Bonaccorso gains great joy out of participating. Consequently, any participation model to be developed in the coming chapters must avoid focusing on noninstrumental returns in isolation, but explore, more precisely, how the noninstrumental, expressive, or symbolic dimension may itself be determined by the instrumental domain of strict costs and outcome-oriented benefits.

2.5   IDIOM VERSUS MOTIVATION

Finally, it is important to establish a distinction routinely drawn by social theorists and equally routinely overlooked by rational choice theorists and public opinion specialists. The distinction is central to the theory of expressive choice developed here and carries strong substantive and methodological implications.

If voters are at least in part expressively motivated, then why do citizens in their survey responses provide instrumental justifications for their electoral choices? Voters do not typically justify their actions in existential terms: they do not justify their voting Democrat in terms of their own political (or other) identity, but in terms of the (alleged) electoral consequence of their vote and its subsequent consequence on policy. The *idiom* of their response is instrumentally rational. This in itself, however, is not sufficient to claim that the voter's motivation is instrumental. As in the discussion of jukebox participation, even expressively motivated action will still involve an individual's relating her actions to a collective outcome.

The expressive individual is one who is motivated not by producing outcomes, but by attaching to outcomes. If I vote for my preferred candidate and he wins, I become one of the voters who successfully got that candidate elected. And if my preferred candidate loses, conversely, I can do one of two things. I can attach to the collective of voters that was unsuccessful in getting our preferred candidate elected and thereby identify myself as a nonsupporter of the newly elected official that beat our candidate. (An ostensible and well-known example of such expression is found in a bumper sticker that began circulating the first week after Bill Clinton's election in 1992, reading "Don't Blame Me—I voted for Bush.")[12] Alternatively, I can lie about whom I voted for, as voters evidently do after the result of an election is known (Wright 1990, 1992, 1993). Both are forms of attachment, negative and positive, and both forms of attachment involve expres-

---

[12] Probably the most persuasive approach to political expression using buttons and bumper stickers is found in Noelle-Neuman (1993).

sion. The *idiom* of expression in either case, however, is instrumental in that the voter still relates the act of voting to the result of an election's. This would indicate that regardless of whether your personal Democratness is guided by a strategic calculation (necessarily a miscalculation) that you want to effect a change in social welfare policy, or by a desire to be someone who cares about welfare policy, your response to survey questions, including Why do you vote? would be identical. Idiom, therefore, is a poor reflection of motivation, and this, of course, has severe implications for the use of surveys or opinion polls to identify voter motivation. As I argue in the historical account of chapter five, we derive better supportive evidence for expressive motivation by using as proxy evidence producers' expressively focused marketing and campaign strategy.

2.6 CONCLUSION

In this chapter I outlined the features of what I introduced as "jukebox" participation and began projecting them onto the wider sphere of electoral and market mass participation. In particular, I concentrated on those characteristics that lie counter to the instrumental components of individuals' motivation to participate in large-scale electoral settings. I concentrate on these characteristics because they represent a suitable starting point for an analysis attempting to identify and characterize noninstrumental participant motivation. My approach in this book is motivated by a perceived need to move the explanation beyond the standard instrumental framework that characterizes much of current rational choice work. My emphasis in this chapter, and throughout the remainder of this book, however, is on not losing sight of the instrumental context altogether. There are several reasons for this.

First, as the example of Bonaccorso demonstrates, the instrumental and expressive components of participant motivation may well be related and should, therefore, not be treated in isolation: in Bonaccorso's case, a high cost of participation in fact *raised* the noninstrumental benefits he appeared to derive out of participation. If in addition to the outcome-oriented Doing-dimension there is an interpretive, identity-based Being-dimension, and if therefore the act of participation is both a source and a signal, to the Self and to others, of *who* the participant *is*, then the price paid (and seen to be paid) for such participation will in itself determine its value to the participant. As we have seen in Bonaccorso's case, to reduce his *cost* of attending the concert is to reduce the *value* to him of attending the concert.

A second reason for not sacrificing the instrumental dimension while pursuing the expressive component of participants' motivation is that, as I will show in part two, producers target both dimensions of individual participant motivation, and to target one will have very direct effects on the other. As noted in the previous chapter, Bush in his presidential campaign appealed to prospective voters along both lines simultaneously. First, his appeal, much in accordance with our identified "jukebox" strategy, communicated that his candidacy was supported by a majority of the voting public and, as was true for most of his campaign, he did not describe the identity characteristics of that alleged majority. In our current terms, he combined our jukebox's "claiming popularity" dimension with its "horizontal shielding of fellow participants." At the same time, however, with the separation of a few sentences, Bush also urged prospective members of that alleged anonymous majority in fact to participate, by stating that their participation was crucial to his attaining electoral victory—an apparent contradiction to the first claim. In the terms established so far, Bush's emphasis on imminent victory targets prospective participants' expressive component, whereas his emphasis on stressing the instrumental importance of every individual vote targets the outcome-oriented component. What is most fascinating, as the formal analysis of chapter seven will show, is that the combination of the expressive and the instrumental contains a delicate strategic balancing act. As I will formally demonstrate, to stress the instrumental always and inevitably will be to undermine the expressive.

And, finally, a third reason why the expressive dimension should not be treated in isolation from the instrumental dimension is that the idiom of justification quite typically is instrumental. The issue of interpreting surveyed respondents' stated explanations for their participation poses great difficulty to researchers to the present day (e.g., Verba, Schlozman, and Brady 1995), and is "old hat" to social science in general.[13] The simple realization that human motivation is sufficiently complex and is likely to run on more than one motivational "fuel" is sufficiently close to a truism for the statement itself to be trivial. Much of my focus, consequently, will rest on how expressive motivation and instrumental idiom typically represent two sides of the same coin.

[13] Frazer's *Golden Bough* ([1922] 1940) is an early illustration of how ethnography has difficulty in dealing with the ritual realities of tribal cultures. Members of one tribe responded to an ethnographer's question about why they were partaking in a particular activity by stating that they were fish. Frazer did not distinguish between idiom and actual reason and reported that members of the tribe in question thought they were fish.

Chapter Three

THEORETICAL FRAME 1: CHOICE AND DOING

> It's no good running a pig farm for thirty years
> while saying "I was meant to be a ballet dancer." By
> that time pigs are your style.
> *(Quentin Crisp)*

> It's not that chewing gum undermines metaphysics but
> that it is metaphysics—this is what must be made clear.
> *(Leo Lowenthal)*

> *Be* original: *drink* Dr Pepper!
> *(Advertisement)*

THE BRITISH anthropologist and philosopher Ernest Gellner once remarked: "It is a curious but indisputable fact that every philosophical baby that is born alive is either a little positivist or a little Hegelian" (1985, 4). Similarly, Jon Elster comments: "One of the most persistent cleavages in the social sciences is the opposition between two lines of thought conveniently associated with Adam Smith and Emile Durkheim, between *homo economicus* and *homo sociologicus*" (1989b, 99). In these stylized terms, the present work attempts to expand the side traditionally identified as "positivist" by adding a "Hegelian" flavor, or the side normally associated with "economicus" by adding some "sociologicus" considerations. In terms of the language first introduced in the previous chapter, the task is to construct a theoretical microfoundation that adds to the Doing dimension of participants' motivation a more deeply rooted dimension of Being.

The three opening quotations are taken from a social critic and performance artist, from a prominent voice of the twentieth-century Continental philosophical tradition of what came to be known as the Frankfurt School, and from an advertising campaign of a well-known soft drink manufacturer (Crisp 1987; Jay 1996). These three highly divergent voices share a focus on activity as a source of social identity. *Doing* pig farming contradicts *being* a ballet dancer. *Doing* gum chewing, analytically, defines the chewer's *being* and thus represents a valid—in this particular case, critical—object of philosophical inquiry. The advertised persuasion to *do* Dr Pepper drinking is justified by its alleged consequence for the participant of *being* original. Despite the great contextual variety of these settings, and of the theoretical orientation of their authors, in all three cases an existential dimension is tied closely to an instrumental one. In the first two cases, this occurs in the context of social commentary, critique, and criticism, and in the third it is applied in a producer's strategic efforts to elicit participation among prospective consumers.[1]

In this chapter and the next I construct a theoretical framing of the argument in this book. I note that although existing economic approaches have been very successful in modeling outcome-oriented, or instrumental, human behavior, to date they have been quite unsuccessful in approaching symbolic or expressive behavior. The first realm is that of *Doing*—individuals perform X in order to *do Y*—and the second is that of identification, attachment, or *Being*—individuals perform X as this is how they *become X*-performers. Alternatively, Doing falls into Max Weber's domain of "formal rationality," whereas Being belongs to his "value" or "substantive rationality" (Weber 1978). I argue that rational choice theorists have had such limited success in modeling the behavior of voters in large-scale elections because they have attempted to approach behavior motivated by Being with tools designed to study Doing. This limitation is well illustrated through a review of the literature on voter turnout and voter choice: it is well-known that rational choice approaches to voter *turnout* have been plagued by the collective action problem, and, as I will demonstrate in this chapter, it is easily shown that rational choice approaches to voter *choice* have actually worsened the paradox of turnout.

In reviewing the solutions that theorists have proposed in response to the collective action problem, I begin with those responses that have suggested a slight reformulation of voters' instrumental returns to participation through inclusion of some noninstrumental utility terms (originally Riker and Ordeshook 1968); I continue with theorists who have proposed somewhat more dramatically that an altogether different, albeit still instrumentally based, voter decision-making model might underlie electoral participation, and that voting consequently should be approached using a different decision theory (originally Ferejohn and Fiorina [1974, 1975] and Ledyard [1984]); and I end with the call by various theorists for an altogether different ap-

---

[1] That the consumption illustration is taken from soft drink marketing is not as arbitrary as one might think: as I will review in chapter five, soft drinks represent the first product systematically to have entered a mass market. As such, they also are among the first to be marketed via a strategic targeting of prospective consumers' expressive motivation.

proach, anchored in the domain of "symbolic utility" and "liturgy" (e.g., Brennan and Buchanan 1984; Uhlaner 1989).

In the next chapter—chapter four—I provide a theoretical micro-foundation for such symbolic or expressive motivation. Unlike for most theorists, who assume that to pursue the expressive dimension requires us to forgo an economic approach, I argue that expressively motivated action does in fact lend itself to a systematic incentive-based approach. Drawing on the work of anthropologists, social theorists, and philosophers studying expressive (or, as they tend to call it, symbolic) action, I identify three determinants of expressive value. The first of these involves the role of symbolic ambiguity and poly-semy (or multivocality), and the second and third determinants of expressive value are both anchored in the realm of "normal" practice. The former identifies the capacity of symbols to generate multiple meanings, and the latter two note (following anthropologists) how an act's symbolic meaning is determined, first, by *who* is performing the act, and, second, by *how many* are performing that act. These three determinants lend themselves to formalization, which will permit me, in future chapters, to formulate a logic of expressive choice.

3.1 TURNOUT

Rational choice theorists studying electoral choice have been able to do so only if they assume there to be turnout. As I now show through a review of the turnout and choice literature, the very rationality these theorists ascribe to voters' choosing among candidates makes these same voters' electoral participation more paradoxical still.

Political scientists in the United States, perhaps more so than any-where else, are fascinated with citizen participation in elections. This persistent interest has both substantive and analytical grounds, even though they tend to pull scholars in opposite directions. Substantive approaches tend to question why electoral participation is so low, whereas analytical approaches tend to question why it should be so high.

On the one hand, American political scientists hold a strong sub-stantive interest in electoral turnout, because participation levels are lower in the United States than they are in other developed de-mocracies. Turnout in presidential elections has reduced steadily over time from 1960 when an already low 63 percent of the population of eligible voters participated in the national election, to 1996, when less than 50 percent participated. Participation rates in midterm elections hover around an even less impressive 35 percent (Rosenstone and

Hansen 1993, 57). This compares with a steady range of 70–95 percent in the countries of Western Europe, with the exception consistently of Switzerland, and occasionally of France, in the same time period.[2] Italy, for example, has less governmental stability and therefore many more elections per year than either its European Union partners or the United States. Additionally, it has public elections for many more different types of office. Yet despite the significantly greater number of opportunities for citizens to participate, and despite the short-livedness of electorally determined outcomes, Italian participation rates in national elections almost always lie in the range of 90–94 percent. Similar contrasting statistics can be found for other forms of political participation, including among interest groups and citizen grassroot movements.[3] Substantively, therefore, participation is of interest to American political scientists, because participation levels in the United States are particularly low and as such go against the grain of democratic representation. The response of the discipline since the 1960s has been a great amount of empirical research—initially at Columbia and Michigan, and soon thereafter essentially everywhere else—to identify in great detail the likely determinants of electoral turnout.

Interestingly, if the substantive interest in turnout is driven by low participation rates, the focus of political scientists concerned with the analytical dimensions of electoral turnout is based on puzzlement as to why participation rates should be as high as they are. For reasons I previewed in the opening chapter and will now investigate in greater detail, analytical approaches driven by collective action or public-good theory predict widespread abstention and free-riding in elections. It is for this reason that participation is considered "paradoxical."

3.1.1 The Paradox of Participation

The "paradox of participation" stands at the center of rational choice approaches to collectives. In part tracing its roots to Mancur Olson's

---

[2] The range is calculated from statistics of Mackie and Rose's *International Almanac of Electoral History*. Participation in national parliamentary elections in Switzerland in the 1980s has dropped below 50 percent.

[3] The story is actually a little more complicated, in that, from a "production" perspective, there are many more interest groups per capita in the United States than there are in Europe (Berry 1989; Walker 1991), although in Europe, citizen engagement to a much larger degree is incorporated into political parties: unions are active within Britain's Labor party, and the four major parties in Germany all contain sections for specialized interests, such as women and youth, for instance. Yet the level of engagement among the citizenry, regardless of whether they organize outside the party or within it, is higher in Europe than it is in the United States.

original work on interest groups (1965), this paradox, or the "problem of collective action," has come to be central not only there, but in instances involving the production of public goods more generally. Olson himself originally drew on the work of economists like Paul Samuelson (1954, 1955, 1958) and provided a model that explained why, at the time of his writing, there was a marked absence of interest-group activity.

Olson's familiar argument is that interest groups produce outcomes that are of benefit, not only to those that effect those outcomes (interest-group members), but also to those that play no part in producing these outcomes. The policy arena sets us squarely in the realm of public goods, because the outcomes produced by interest groups are nonexcludable: producers and nonproducers alike are able to partake in the resultant benefits. The costs associated with bringing about those benefits, however, are faced only by those who choose to participate in the group's activities: in other words, if benefits are wholly public and nonexcludable, the costs of production in contrast are private and borne only by the participants.

Consequently, in large groups, potential participants have no incentives to accept participation costs because they receive the benefits of collective action regardless of whether they themselves participate in that action. In Olson's terms, and as I suggested earlier, rational individuals face strong incentives to "free-ride" on others' activities. Furthermore, if it is irrational for one individual to participate, it is irrational for all individuals to participate.[4] The collective action problem is a problem precisely because individual rationality "irrationally" undermines groups' activities (Barry and Hardin 1982): if individuals, on the whole, prefer the existence of the group to its nonexistence, even if this were to involve a private cost of participation, the presence of free-rider, or "perverse," incentives would prevent individuals' participation once the group is formed, thus leading to its unraveling.

Olson focused on a set of conditions under which participation was most likely to occur. Chief among these are considerations of group size and the presence of what he called "selective incentives." Incentives are selective if "those who do not join the organization working for the group's interest, or in other ways contribute to the attainment of the group's interest, can be treated differently from those who do"

[4] Unless, of course, some individuals decide to participate precisely because they expect others will not participate. In an election this expectation would lead you to assume that your vote would be decisive. This in itself, of course, would once again motivate everybody to participate, although then your vote would become indecisive. This back-and-forth logic is contained in a general-equilibrium model presented by Ledyard (1984).

(1965, 51). Olson additionally noted that a persistent theme in the history of social groups is that, when compared to large groups, smaller groups are more likely to persist over time.[5] Both economic and social incentives were said to be responsible for that empirical regularity.

Economically, small groups provide greater returns to individual action, in that both the individual's share of the public good, as well as the individual's *instrumental* responsibility of bringing about that public good, are increased:[6]

> In a small group in which a member gets such a large fraction of the total benefit that he would be better off if he paid the entire cost himself, rather than go without the good, there is some presumption that the collective good will be provided. In a group in which no one member got such a large benefit from the collective good that he had an interest in providing it even if he had to pay all of the cost, but to which the individual was still so important in terms of the whole group that his contribution or lack of contribution to the group objective had a noticeable effect on the costs or benefits of others in the group, the result is indeterminate. (1965, 44)

Participating in the activities of small groups reflects a reduced ratio of privately borne cost to privately (as opposed to publicly) accrued returns to individual action. In addition, small groups provide greater social pressures and incentives to contribute, through intragroup friendships and the like, because small groups tend to provide a less anonymous environment than large groups. Small groups, in Olson's analysis, therefore either provide greater net benefits to individuals, as they are responsible for a larger share of the public good, or they provide additional small-group-specific enticements in the form of social incentives that large groups are unable to provide to those participating individuals.

Finally, it is interesting to note that some selective incentives emerge directly from group size, whereas others do not. Returns to participation such as social status, personal prestige, and self-esteem

---

[5] Olson cites Kurt Wolff's translation of *The Sociology of Georg Simmel* and George Homans's *The Human Group* for evidence (Olson 1965, 53–65).

[6] The notion of an "individual's share" of a public good is in itself problematic in that public-good consumption is by definition nonrival. This is further complicated by the fact that Olson is somewhat inconsistent in his definition and use of "small groups" and "privileged groups," and consequently in defining the exact boundaries of the collective of beneficiaries of a public good. As the following quote suggests, however, Olson's notion of a share, in this context, relates not to rivalness in consumption, but to relative valuation by some members of the group as opposed to others. If that is the case, however, it remains questionable as to how an individual's likelihood to participate directly depends on the size of the group.

are particularly prevalent in smaller groups. Other, more tangible, returns are size independent and include the distribution of private membership benefits as diverse as the receipt of interest-group membership magazines and invitations to annual banquets (Berry 1989; Walker 1991; Lowry 1993).

3.1.2 The Paradox Made Worse: Elections

Olson addressed citizen participation in interest groups. The very same logic and its prediction of nonparticipation are easily transposed to the electoral context. Here, in fact, participation appears to be more paradoxical still.

To begin with, in Olson's public-good setting of interest groups, individuals' participation can in fact improve the quality of the public good: taking into account, for example, that the individual's lack of participation will itself, however minutely, lower the probability of the good's provision, and taking into account, more significantly, that the value of the provided good may itself decrease in the absence of the individual's participation, nonparticipation may in fact be said only to provide a ride that is *cheap*, not free.[7] This point is raised by Stigler (1974) and is relevant as we turn our focus to Olson and elections: we know that the impact of the individual's vote on the electoral outcome with virtual certainty will be indistinguishable from zero. More relevantly, we also know that the value or quality of the outcome itself remains unchanged: in the context of majority-rule elections, and in contrast to public goods provided by interest groups, the *level* of provision will not change in the absence of the individual's participation. The value of the outcome is dichotomous, and any one individual's contribution, subsequently, is even more thoroughly irrelevant in elections than it is in the activities of interest groups. Elections, consequently, are an even starker instance of the collective action problem.

Similarly, the vast size of the electorate—or even of the proportion of the electorate supporting a particular candidate—indicates an absence of small-group-specific incentives to participate. Admittedly, the boundaries of the relevant group are not necessarily prescribed in electorate terms. Many theorists who have provided "solidary-incen-

---

[7] In expected-value analytical terms, both scenarios are identical: the first notes a lowering of the *probability* of a good's provision; the second notes a lowering of the *value* of the provided good. "Expected value" is the product of the probability of generating an outcome and the value of the generated outcome. Both bases to the "cheap ride" argument, consequently, are identical in that both amount to a reduction in the expected value of participation.

tive" arguments have described local associations down to the neighborhood, kinship, or household levels as providing the relevant returns to participation: it may be the fact that your electoral participation pleases your mother or your friends at the local bridge club that motivates you to participate, rather than any impact you may have on the election. However, this type of argument constitutes a break with strict outcome-oriented reasoning, as it situates the latent motivation outside the manifest consequence of the electoral act. As I shall show, such relocation warrants theoretical grounding and a great deal of caution, so as not to reduce itself to poor tautological reasoning. For now, however, it should be noted only that what both the public-good and small-group arguments indicate is that the Olsonian response to Olson's original puzzle almost exclusively has focused on seeking out other sources of incentives that selectively discriminate between participants and nonparticipants.

Finally, before turning our attention to electoral choice and its impact on the participation paradox, it should be noted that the collective action problem is accompanied by another well-known paradox introduced by Downs: if, indeed, voters have no impact on the election, why should they inform themselves about the value of the candidates? Information gathering is costly. Why face this cost if it cannot be applied to shape the outcome of the election? If voters face a dominant incentive to abstain from electoral participation, similarly they face a dominant incentive rationally to remain ignorant (Downs 1957). As I will show, the types of responses to the observation that people do in fact gather information when we predict them not to typically have been similar to responses to the observation that people do in fact participate in elections when our analytical prediction is that they will not. Once we can identify reasons why voters participate in elections, more than likely we can then point to the same reasons explaining why it is that they become informed about candidates.

3.2 CHOICE

Downs's "rational ignorance" paradox is relevant in a broader sense. It shows how the paradox of participation logically ripples out to other realms of electoral decision making and generates other paradoxes there. Indeed, once stated in the form of "rational ignorance," this consequentialist pursuit and extension of the collective action problem should strike us as obvious enough. All the more perplexing, therefore, that the paradox of electoral *turnout* has been ignored entirely by theorists studying electoral *choice*. As I now turn to discuss, theories of choice at best have had to assume turnout, as they have been incapable of explaining it. At worst, choice theories have in fact worsened the participation paradox, as their approach to choice makes turnout more paradoxical still. I focus on two prevalent political economy approaches to electoral choice: spatial models and information externality models of choice.

3.2.1 Spatial Models of Choice

Downs's greatest contribution was the formulation of spatial models of electoral choice. Drawing on the work of Harold Hotelling (1990), Downs proposed an ideological choice dimension over which an electorate's preferences are distributed, and along which candidates situate themselves so as to maximize electoral support. The famous result, or prediction, is that of the median voter theorem (MVT): in the single-dimensional, two-candidate case, both candidates will converge at the ideological position of the median voter. The result changes as the number of candidates increases (for example, in the single-dimensional case it is indeterminate with three candidates and becomes determinate again with four candidates),[8] and becomes "chaotic" as the number of choice dimension becomes greater than one.[9] Much of the spatial literature since Downs has focused on the nature of multidimensional spatial logic and on the role of institutions and party conflict in determining equilibria (Shepsle 1979, 1989; Shepsle and Weingast 1981).

It is crucial to note that Downs's original formulation of spatial competition occurred in the electoral context, although many successful spatial applications since have been made in the context of legislative decision making. Technically, the distinction between these two realms of application can be a subtle one, as evidenced by theorists' straight forward application of one and the same methodological tool in either context. Substantively, however, the use of spatial models in

---

[8] For a full review of the spatial literature, as well as the results generated in the multicandidate and multidimensional case, see Shepsle (1991).

[9] McKelvey's chaos theorem (1979) states that in the multidimensional setting, any status quo can be beaten by another point that is preferred by a majority, which in turn of course can also be beaten by yet another point. In fact, "chaos" emerges from the fact that any outcome can be derived from any starting point through a finite number of sequential votes using majority rule. This condition holds unless voters' ideal points line up in a very specific manner satisfying Plott's "radial symmetry" condition. Radial symmetry essentially reduces the geometry of the multidimensional setting to a single-dimensional one. For a clear and simple overview of this logic and its conditions, see Shepsle and Bonchek (1997, 101).

the electoral context generates specific problems, for it is in the electoral context that spatial arguments have to face and overcome the collective action problem.

As noted, spatial theorists assume that candidates know and respond to the distribution of voters' preferences and place themselves so as to minimize their relative distance from a maximum number of voters. This implies that voters will know this distribution, too: they will hold this information directly, or at the very least they will be able to infer it from the strategic positioning of the candidates. *However, if voters know where they themselves stand relative to the rest of the electorate, they should also know what the outcome of the election will be and, consequently, whether their own vote will be redundant or insufficient in bringing about the desired electoral result.* Spatial models of choice in the electoral context, based on rational decision making, are successful only if they remain agnostic about the rationality of turnout. In practice they require that one set of motivations guides the voter to the polling booth, whereas a different set of motivations will drive the voters once they are inside the booth.

This assumption, substantively, is an odd one and quite different from the assumption of theorists studying individual choice elsewhere. For example, economists studying consumer behavior will not typically assume that consumers decide, first, that they require a good, and second, that this good be flour: consumers go to the store (that is, they turn out) *because* they want flour. It is the preference for flour that seamlessly guides both the consumer's trip to the grocery store, and his selection of flour over scouring powder. In the context of consumption, it would be utterly absurd to assume that motivation guiding participation and choice could be separated. Why should it be any different in the case of voting, even if to do so is an analytical requirement for a particular class of choice models to work?

3.2.2   Information Externality Models of Choice

If spatial models of choice require us to be agnostic about the rationality of turnout, the other dominant model of choice—information externality models—more dramatically requires us to be antirational in our assumptions underlying such turnout.

Several theorists have drawn on the work of Industrial Organization (IO) theorists and argued that voters look at the vote intentions of other voters in order to inform themselves about the likely quality of the candidates (e.g., Bikhchandani, Hirshleifer, and Welch 1992; Bartels 1988). These approaches are based on the assumption that voters rationally take cost-saving shortcuts: rather than face the cost of informing yourself about candidate quality, you rely on cheaper proxy evidence of others' expected voting to form your own vote choice. This proxy is the external consequence of others' support for the candidate—hence the term "externality." The more voters are seen to support a candidate, the better that candidate must be: 80 percent of the population simply cannot be wrong.

One obvious consequence of such information-externality choice formation is that it generates electoral and public-opinion bandwagons: if visible popular support generates further support for a candidate, then we would expect there to be electoral bandwagons extending, for example, over primaries in presidential campaigns (Bartels 1988). Alternatively, information-externality bandwagons may extend over public opinion polls published in the media in the time leading up to an election (Herbst 1993).

A perverse consequence of the aggregation of individuals' proxy reasoning is that the generated bandwagons need not be efficient, in that they do not necessarily support the superior candidate or product: contrary to the individual voter's alleged reasoning, 80 percent of the population *can* in fact very well be wrong! The best-known examples in the product-based IO literature are those of VHS video standards, which "bandwagoned" out the qualitatively superior Beta standard of early video recorders, because they had an early head start in manufacturers' competition for an industrial standard; of early Intel-based computer operating systems that crowded out early and then-superior Macintosh platform operating systems; and early QWERTY-configuration typing keyboards (named after the upper left six keys of a typewriter), which initially were adapted precisely because their configuration of keys made typewriters user *un*friendly. Early typewriters could not handle fast typing speeds: consequently keys were arranged in a manner so as to slow down the typist. The resultant norm or standard has ensured that, today, the planet's population of alphanumeric typists is locked into using an inefficient and inferior keyboard standard.

Similarly, in the electoral context, econometric models such as Bartels's have shown how presidential campaigns like Jimmy Carter's in 1976 initially got off the ground and ultimately led to electoral victory through a strategic stacking, in Carter's favor, of the straw polls prior to the early New Hampshire primary. Whether that particular election produced the best possible president is obviously irrelevant to the argument here. What matters is that the dynamic by which the candidate becomes and remains a front-runner need not relate to the candidate's qualities, if the world of choice is driven by information externalities.

The microfoundations of information-externality approaches, in a narrow sense, appear to represent a suitable response to Downs's "rational ignorance" puzzle: voters do not become independently informed, but rely on cheaper proxy evidence of others' vote intentions. In a much broader sense, however, the instrumental foundation of information-externality models is fiercely at odds with rational turnout. For if voters draw on the voting behavior of others in their assessment of a candidate's quality, then they should also draw on the very same information to conclude that their own vote is utterly irrelevant to the outcome of the election. To know that 60 percent of a population is voting for a candidate is to know *with certainty* the redundancy or insufficiency of your own vote. Once again, the careful sophistication that is said to motivate voters' choice among candidates necessarily is absent when these voters decide whether to participate in the election. This, to be sure, is not to deny that bandwagons exist—as future chapters will reveal, an expressively based approach in fact generates a prediction of collective-level bandwagons. It is, however, to question the very microfoundation that information-externality choice theorists claim is responsible for them.

For both spatial and information-externality theorists, the instrumental rationality of choice, substantively, is in contradiction to an instrumental rationality of turnout. Both require us to assume that one flavor of motivation guides the voter to the voting booth, whereas another guides her once she is there. Yet, as I will show, the method proposed by these theorists is still useful: in fact, much of the analysis to be introduced in chapter six of this book will posit noninstrumental information externalities and generate predictions concerning electoral bandwagons and the like. The theoretical microfoundations, and the analytical specifications of the models to be developed, will differ. Most significantly, unlike the approaches reviewed here, the current approach no longer requires us to make inconsistent assumptions across turnout and choice. As I now turn to discuss, initially through a review of different types of responses generated by the paradox of participation, and then by turning to the relevant literature in anthropology and social theory in the next chapter, this inconsistency is removed if we put in place an expressively based microfoundation.

3.3 RESPONSES TO THE PARTICIPATION PARADOX

The discussion of turnout and choice has revealed that the extent of an individual vote's irrelevance to an electoral result will be a function both of the size of the electorate and the closeness of the vote intentions of all other voters. Some theorists have noted that in large-scale elections, closeness subsequently might explain electoral turnout in perfectly consistent instrumental terms. This, however, is necessarily false: for example, simple statistical approximation shows that for an electorate of 100 million participating voters, wherein every voter is stylized to vote according to a coin toss, and wherein the tossed coin is biased toward one of the candidates by the very small weight of 0.001, the probability of casting a decisive vote carries, roughly, a 1 in 12^{15} magnitude.[10] The instrumental benefit of individual participation in terms of bringing about a preferred outcome remains essentially at zero, even if the election is significantly closer than it has ever been in any presidential election in the history of the United States. Perfectly in line with the participation paradox, this benefit consequently is outweighed by the cost of voting, even if the latter is measured singularly by the probability of getting killed in a road accident on the way to the voting booth. Closeness simply cannot provide a sufficient reason in outcome-oriented terms, if the election is a large one.

The literature has responded to the participation paradox in various ways. The purpose here is not to provide detailed inventory of these responses, but to establish three classes under which these responses fall. This classification will enable us to situate my approach in this book, which shares aspects with each of them.

3.3.1   Selective Incentives

One type of response to the paradox of participation has noted that individuals might be motivated by tangible and intangible selective incentives. This, of course, is a strict Olsonian response. If the outcome of the election is not within voters' instrumental reach, they must be motivated by some incentives that, quite possibly, are unrelated to that outcome. Benefits, accordingly, are not determined prob-

---

[10] This value is obtained by estimating the probability of a tie occurring if there are an even number of other voters (Brennan and Buchanan 1984) and multiplying that value by 0.5 because this is the probability that the number of other voters is even. Consequently, the probability of the marginal voter having an effect on the outcome of an election involving n voters is

$$p = \frac{1}{2} \left(\frac{N}{\frac{N}{2}} \right) q^{\frac{N}{2}} (1 - q)^{\frac{N}{2}}$$

where q is the probability of other voters voting for one candidate over another.

abilistically in terms of the success of affecting (that is, effecting) an electoral result.

One variant of selective-incentive-based reasoning is found in moral or civic-duty arguments. These approaches typically posit that at least part of the population, relative to the option of free-riding, will ask, "What if everybody thought this way?" What if everybody were to think only of his or her private net benefits in deciding whether to participate in the election? There would be no public good, no civic product. Incidentally, as is well-known, this claim was brought forward in the democratic theory of Truman (1951) and Dahl (1963), before the collective action problem was formulated in the literature, and only later came to be reintegrated as a response to the participation paradox. Civic-duty arguments have also played a central role in the empirically focused Michigan School approaches to electoral behavior (e.g., Verba and Nie 1972). Influenced by the tradition of Dahl's distinction between *homo civicus* and *homo politicus*, political scientists attempt to measure what types of citizens are most likely to participate in the election.

The first, and perhaps still best-known, analytical incarnation of civic-duty arguments is found in Riker and Ordeshook's famous paper of 1968.[11] Beginning with a basic returns-to-participation utility function $R_i = pB_i - C$, Riker and Ordeshook note how p—the probability of determining the electoral outcome—quickly diminishes toward zero as the size of the electorate becomes large.[12] The expected-value benefit term pB_i, consequently, also decreases toward zero and therefore quickly will be outweighed by the cost-of-participation term C. If, however, voters are motivated, say, by a sense of civic duty, then this should be added to the utility function, which subsequently will read $R_i = pB_i - C + D$. Provided that $pB_i + D > C$ for the individual voter (which implies that the benefits of participation outweigh the costs), she will participate in the election. The substance of this type of explanation is in itself consistent with the approach of this book, in that the expressive approach, too, posits a private return to participation that is not strictly dependent on the electoral outcome. However, in Riker and Ordeshook's original form, and in today's var-

---

[11] It may seem odd critically to address an article of over thirty years ago. That this criticism is still a valid characterization of attempts at including a noninstrumental motivation today is reflected in current debates on the present state of the literature (e.g., Aldrich 1997).

[12] The term B contains the subscript i as it is determined by the difference between the individual voter's utility for the preferred candidate relative to her utility for the alternate candidate. As preferences for candidates will differ for different voters i, both B and the summed utility term R will carry the subscript.

ious incarnations of their argument, this type of approach does carry some important shortcomings.

First, such an approach tends to be the product of failed collective action theory: it is because pure outcome-oriented factors fail to carry the story that non-outcome-oriented factors are slowly allowed into it. The emphasis of explanation, consequently, will carry an inherent tilt toward the instrumental side. Second, this type of gradual explanatory expansion up to the point of explanatory "success" makes for bad theory, not just because of the inherent bias toward the instrumental, but because little is in fact *explained*: to continue to add factors to a model until it is consistent with whatever findings are of interest is in itself atheoretical, as everything, eventually, can be "explained" (or, rather, allowed for) that way. If we do allow for non-outcome-related incentives to enter the equation, especially if these are intangible noninstrumental incentives, then these must be approached in as comprehensive a manner as we have come to analyze the economy of instrumental incentives that typically are said to guide voters and other participants in public goods. Merely to add a static term to the equation—*even if the term substantively is a correct one*—reduces its purpose to that of a "sponge"—or as Ferejohn and Fiorina call it, a "catch-all"—term (1974, 535).

In Olsonian terms, the incentives I seek in this book are "selective" in that they accrue to those who participate. The incentives are intangible as they are not directly measurable. Unlike in existing approaches, however, these terms are not invariant, nor are they aberrations from instrumental or outcome-oriented incentives. Instead they can be shown to form a coherent logic of choice.

3.3.2 Alternative Decision Criteria

It cannot be overemphasized that the criterion of instrumental rationality upon which the collective action problem is based applies a single, very specific decision rule founded on expected-value calculations. There is nothing either analytically neutral or substantively natural about this criterion: according to collective action theory, prospective voters are deterred from participating in the election because they are thought to compare the cost of participation to the *expected benefit* generated by their participation. To apply expected-value terms analytically, however, is in itself to make a substantive judgment, because other instrumental decision criteria exist. For example, in a well-known approach, Ferejohn and Fiorina (1974, 1975) relocate the question of turnout by moving it from the standard formal terms of "decision making under risk" to an approach analytically grounded in terms of "decision making under uncertainty." Here they apply Savage's minimax regret criterion, a decision rule formulated not in terms of maximizing the expected value of a desired outcome, but in terms of minimizing the magnitude of a possible (even if unlikely) undesired outcome. The voter is characterized not as asking how great an impact her participation is likely to have on the collective outcome, but instead as asking, "My God, what if I didn't vote and my preferred candidate lost by one vote? I'd feel like killing myself" (Ferejohn and Fiorina 1975, 535). Minimax regret criteria address not the probability of an event occurring, but the mere possibility that an undesired event might occur. This formal approach provides an outcome substantially different from that of conventional approaches to participation: "Our comparison of expected utility maximization and minimax regret decision criteria shows that the behavior of decision makers using the alternative rules differs considerably. Specifically, expected utility maximizers go to the polls only under the most restrictive conditions, whereas minimax regret decision makers need little incentive to participate. And one should remember that most people vote."

Regardless of whether we see minimax-regret decision rule substantively as plausible, Ferejohn and Fiorina's objection is highly relevant to the present analysis. It emphasizes that there is no single decision metric to be applied in rational choice investigation: the choice of modus is itself of substantive relevance and has direct analytical consequences. The paradox of participation, therefore, is closely tied not just to the assumption of instrumental rationality, but to the assumption of expected-value instrumental rationality. Previously I referred to approaches that *substantively* seek other benefits to explain why there is participation in the production of public goods. The present category of responses refers to substantively motivated approaches that ask how benefits *analytically* factor into individuals' decision rule. Ferejohn and Fiorina's use of a different decision rule is just one powerful example that shows the volatility of the analytical result relative to its decision-rule assumptions.

Another illustration of this volatility is found in a well-known argument by Ledyard (1984) that voters reason in general-equilibrium terms. If voters individually base their decision rule on expected-value calculations, it follows that they individually assess the probability of their vote creating or breaking a tie in the election. If they are rational, then they should assume that other voters, too, will make their decisions in the same manner. As Ledyard has shown, this can be sufficient to move the predicted equilibrium condition of turnout away from an expected electoral outcome of zero: voters will reason that if all voters were to think this way, nobody would vote, thus generating a tie, at which point the individual's vote would determine the entire election. However, all voters will be aware of this, of course, and thus will wish to participate. Then again, they will know that all voters know this, and will therefore again wish to abstain, and so on: "Somewhere between no one voting and everyone voting lies a situation in which some vote and in which the probability of a tie is consistent with those numbers and with the beliefs of all voters" (1984, 13). In other words, there exists an equilibrium for which between 0 and 100 percent of the population participate in the election.

Unfortunately, Ledyard's model is highly nonrobust in that it is capable of predicting any level of participation in the interval from 0 percent to 100 percent. The model has found more robust applications in nonelectoral public-good settings, wherein benefits of participation are not as inextricably bound to the majority point, such as in citizen participation in political demonstrations (Lohmann 1991a, 1991b). This type of general-equilibrium approach, whereby voters take into account what other voters are likely to do (unlike in partial-equilibrium approaches, whereby voters are assumed to treat population parameters as given), is of substantive interest because it bears a semblance to the civic-duty question, What if everybody thought this way? Here voters assume that everybody else *is* thinking in a similar way, and this factors into their own decision to vote. However, unlike for democratic theorists, who assume that considerations of others' actions are guided by concerns of moral or civic principle, for general-equilibrium theorists such thinking is strategic. For these theorists, individual voters are still rationally concerned with the electoral consequences of their participation. It is therefore still the outcome that motivates the voter, and it is the (expected) degree of participation among other prospective voters that determines the (expected) efficacy of her vote.

The purpose here is not to discuss specific implications of these two responses, especially because much of this discussion has already taken place in the literature (e.g., Goodin and Roberts 1975; Aldrich 1997). Instead, it is to note how these, as well as other, responses to the paradox of participation have attempted to solve the voting paradox by means of redefining the formal basis to decision making. In this context, it is particularly relevant to note that both Ledyard's and Ferejohn and Fiorina's contributions not only respond to the insufficiency of Olson-type approaches to collective action, but react at least as markedly to the earlier response by Riker and Ordeshook previously discussed.

3.3.3 Consumption Benefits

Finally, participating in voting has been compared to audience participation in sporting events (Brennan and Buchanan 1984; Uhlaner 1989). Football fans, for example, in their living rooms may scream at their television sets during game broadcasts, providing players with tactical advice. It is probably safe to assume, however, that these fans know that such screaming in no way will affect the outcome of the game. All the same, they will expend the energy associated with their participation.

What is of relevance, and in perfect accordance with the theoretical point made in the closing of the previous chapter, is that although the *idiom* of participation is one of manipulating the outcome of the sporting event—the fan will instruct the quarterback to pass the ball, or chastise him for having fumbled—the actual *motivation* will not be. The fan will, however, face a cost of participation, and despite his use of an outcome-oriented idiom, his involvement will not be guided by any influence it bears on the outcome of the game. Participation here is therefore not a form of investment, but a form of consumption, as the participant derives value from participation itself.

Consumption benefits are inextricably tied to *expression*: the sports fan's *expression* of team support is required for him to enjoy his participation. Similarly, participation in politics, under a consumption-benefit regime, is inextricably tied to the *expression* of partisanship, or the *expression* of preference toward one of the candidates. Analytically, this involves recasting the very option of participation as a benefit (+), whereas previously it had been considered a cost (−). Albert Hirschman, for example, who had earlier characterized participation in public action to fall along three lines ("exit," "voice," and "loyalty")[13] later notes how he, like other theorists, had perhaps falsely assumed that an act of participation itself necessarily represented a cost. What in the present context I call "expressive," Hirschman refers to as "the use of voice" (Hirschman 1971b, 6): "I allowed myself to be imprisoned by the traditional notion that the use of voice is always costly. My case for the potential superiority of voice over exit would have been considerably strengthened had I realized that in certain situations the use of voice becomes acutely pleasurable and should therefore no longer be computed as a cost, but as a benefit." The difficult question that stands before us now, and will become the

---

[13] "Exit" represents a form of abstention in response to dissatisfaction, whereas "voice" represents an act of attempting to change the (public) source of dissatisfaction. "Loyalty" refers to a state of dissatisfaction coupled with a decision to remain attached all the same (Hirschman 1970).

focus of the next chapter, is why and how expression of preference should constitute a benefit.

3.4 PRELIMINARY CONCLUSION

In the classification of the types of responses to the participation paradox, I have applied a sequence that has increasingly steered us away from the narrow Olsonian setting: I began with the literature which assumes that voters are outcome oriented, but that the relevant outcome resides elsewhere than in the electoral result. I then reviewed approaches that, too, posit outcome-oriented or instrumental rationality, but that question the expected-value, partial-equilibrium decision criteria said to characterize voters' decision making. I subsequently looked at approaches which assumed that voters are not driven by a motivation to generate an outcome in the first place. According to these consumption-based approaches, participation itself generates positive benefits for the participant.

As we move away from the strict Olsonian setting toward consumption-benefit approaches, explanatory responses to the participation paradox become less satisfactory, even if we find them intuitively to ring true. In fact, once we replace the investment notion of participation under an Olsonian incentive regime with the notion of consumption, we essentially risk reducing the status of our approach from explanation to mere description. The collective action question of Why do people participate in the absence of instrumental returns? is synonymous with the question of What benefits do people derive from participation, given that they do not derive any benefits from the ostensible (or manifest) outcome of their action? Simply to posit a consumption benefit is no more than to note that individuals derive benefit from the act of participation. The very definition of this consumption benefit, consequently, is at risk of being no more than the original question of collective action recast as a response.

Stated differently, to note that expression—or "the use of voice"— is pleasurable requires a microlevel theory of incentives. To derive such a microfoundation requires us to look beyond the terms that are typically drawn upon in the context of the collective action literature. I turn to contributions by social theorists, anthropologists, and philosophers, first, to situate logically the source of expressive benefit, and second, to operationalize analytically an economy in which such benefit defines the relevant incentives.

Chapter Four

THEORETICAL FRAME 2: CHOICE AND BEING

> Rational choice modellers will be able to explain voting
> and non-voting as soon as they can solve the problem of
> why people salute the flag when they know that
> nobody is looking.
> *(Bernard Grofman)*

> Every narrative is a discovery/invention, every I that
> expresses itself a narrative.
> *(Max Frisch)*

I N THE PREVIOUS chapter I noted a trend among theorists toward positing a consumption benefit as motivating individuals' participation in collective action. I noted how these accounts typically tied consumption benefit to individuals' expression of preferences. I now look toward a social theoretic microfoundation for such expression. I situate expressive consumption benefit in the realm that, earlier, I identified as "Being." I note how expressive motivation contains a symbolic dimension, in that expressive action is *representative*. I further note that sociologists and social theorists after Max Weber have focused on the role of "Lifestyle," denoting the multitude of choices that characterize and define individuals' daily lives, and how these choices themselves are said to constitute "biographical narratives." They provide and express identity for the decision makers. In accordance with my initial characterization of choice motivated by considerations surrounding Being, individuals' decisions in the theoretical characterization of Lifestyles are motivated by what these decisions *mean* to them and to those around them. This focus on meaning as a source of decision making underlying action portrays individuals as interpretive decision makers.

In this chapter I approach the theoretical microfoundation for expressive choice by tackling three questions. First, if the value of electoral participation for the voter emerges from her understanding of what it means to be voting for a particular candidate, then how is such expressive value generated, and how is it manipulated by candidates and their campaigns?

Second, in the economy of expressive incentives, who are the producers? In Olsonian collective action theory, it is the inability of individuals to produce the collective outcome that results in a failure of collectives to do so. In other words, in the instrumental logic of collective action the failure to generate value for the individual participant prevents a public good from being provided. In a system of expressive incentives, if benefits do not emerge from producing the outcome, who are the agents that are responsible for creating value?

Third, and finally, how do we operationalize expressive incentives? Once we have identified the mechanism by which expressive value emerges, and once we have identified the relevant economic agents, how do we operationalize these features so as to permit us to draw usable predictions?

The first two of these questions can be approached through reference to social theory literature on expressive or symbolic behavior. In particular, I refer to the work of social theorists and anthropologists who are considered to hold an interpretive focus. The third question requires that we bring to bear on this theoretical literature tools derived from simple microeconomics and game theory. If we are to argue for an incentive-based logic of expressive choice, then these appear to be suitable means by which expressive incentives can be approached.

In this chapter, my focus remains theoretical, so that the microfoundation established here (in closing the theoretical part of this book) can be applied in the analytical history of campaigning and marketing, and in its subsequent modeling in part 2.

4.1 EXPRESSIVE MOTIVATION AND SYMBOLIC UTILITY

I begin with the question of the source of expressive value. Expressive motivation by theorists has been tied inextricably to a symbolic dimension. For example, in the context of electoral decision making, Brennan and Buchanan note the "logical gap between voter action and voter preference" (1984, 196). Acccording to them, and in accordance with the expressive claims made here, voting is dependent on the voter's "tastes for showing preferences as such." Such a desire for expression indicates that "voting is to be understood perhaps as 'symbolic' or 'liturgical' (rather like the choice of which team to support in an athletic spectacle) and hardly at all like the choice among alternative investments." For Brennan and Buchanan, the expressive desire to show one's tastes contains a symbolic essence.

Another prominent linking of expression with a symbolic dimension is found in Nozick (1993), who argues that the notion of "symbolic utility" needs to be included in decision theory. As one commentator summarizes this argument, "This amounts to a type of connection between an action and its consequences that concerns not the act's propensity to bring these consequences about, but the way in which the act is regarded as *representing* the valued project of which the action is a component" (Gottlieb 1993). Expression is representative, and thus symbolic. Nozick's focus, consequently, is not on action as a source of utility drawn from causal connections between action and outcome, but as a "symbolic connection" that "enables the action to be expressive of some attitude, belief, value, emotion, or whatever" (Nozick 1993, 28). For Nozick, as for Brennan and Buchanan before him, for action to be expressive requires that it carry a symbolic dimension.

4.1.1 Symbolic Attachment

As I first previewed in the jukebox model in the opening of this book, expressive choice serves as a medium of *attachment*. This is now better understood in the context of symbolic utility.

Attachment exists at two levels. First, in a strictly expressive world voters participate in an election not to create the electoral outcome, but to attach to this outcome. By expressing their preference through their electoral participation, they establish a relationship with the electoral result: one of positive attachment if the result matches their vote (that is, their expressed preference), and one of expressive detachment if it does not.

A second form of attachment that emerges from participation is to the group of fellow participants who are making the same choice. As I noted before, such attachment can be very vague in that the individual Democratic voter may not in fact know many other similarly inclined voters. She will, however, all the same create a sense of attachment with this broad collective, even if for the voter that collective is abstractly and vaguely defined. It is this very attachment, through reference to a collective category, that constitutes Being. Popkin (1991) very eloquently describes this collective dimension by characterizing electoral participation as an act that, for the voter, turns the "I" into a "We."

It is important and interesting to note, however, that although Being draws on a collective or public category (to a "We"), the process of self-identification will seamlessly motivate the individual and her behavior in both public and private. In other words, who that individual *is* is defined in publicly or collectively rooted terms. Once she *is*, however, she *is* equally when she is in public or when she is alone.

To refer to the opening quote of this chapter, there is nothing inherently contradictory, therefore, in saluting a flag while being alone, if such behavior is motivated by a symbolically infused expression of identity. As Grofman famously notes (1983), we could very well expect an identical logic to underlie the symbolically infused expression of identity in voting, or in any other form of political participation.

This type of claim stands on fertile soil in the context of both modern social theory and literature. The notion of Choice as a form of expression, with a symbolic connection, and with an identifying attachment to a larger abstract collective that matters both in public and in private, is perfectly consistent with the idea that individuals' choices constitute "biographical narratives." This idea is captured in literature in expressions such as Max Frisch's in the opening quote to this chapter (which, in its original German, is also the epigraph to this book). Among social theorists, as I now discuss, it is captured in the notion of "Lifestyle."

4.1.2   Expression through "Lifestyle"

Two broad and opposing trends characterize the social theory of expressive behavior in modern social theory. Both of these trace a history back to the sociology of Max Weber. The first includes a focus on modern social life as rationalized, organized, and bureaucratized, wherein this rationalization of society is mirrored in the rationalization of the mind under "modernity." The second trend looks at the increasing role of symbolic expression and identification under "late modernity."

Weber himself saw the institutions of capitalist production and modern bureaucracy as forms of "societal rationalization," involving primarily the rational organization of economic production and of public service respectively (1978). Modernity, in Weber's writings, was to be equated with the advent of the human capacity for rational thought. This capacity itself traces its roots back to the Enlightenment, and capitalist and bureaucratic institutions were its consequent institutional incarnations. For example, where previously there was charismatic leadership, now there were the legal-rational confines of bureaucratic leadership involving the new practices of double-entry bookkeeping, the separation of the means of officeholding from the officeholder, and so forth (1978, 956–58). Such rationalization occurred not only at the level of bureaucratic and capitalist organization, but at the level of mind also: where previously the world had been ruled by colorful magic and religion, now it was seen as ruled by calculating *ratio*. Enlightenment, consequently, according to Weber, came at the cost of "Disenchantment" (*Entzauberung*). In his best-known expression of this condition, in the closing pages of *The Prot-estant Ethic and the Spirit of Capitalism* (1958), Weber notes how instru-mental rationality had placed the human subject in what he gloomily called the "iron cage of modernity."

A trend among continental-European social theorists of the latter half of the twentieth-century has been to note that what might have been true for "early modernity" now no longer holds. The great mul-titude of definitions of the present period in human history (including "postmodernity," "late modernity," "posttradition," and so on) attests both to the great interest in the emerging period, and to the immense fragmentation of the debates that rage in connection with it. Specifi-cally, some scholars associated with the debate take issue with We-ber's "iron cage," not necessarily questioning its historical relevance, but seeking to adapt it to current conditions.

For example, the anthropologist and philosopher Ernest Gellner—an otherwise highly unlikely theorist of late modernity—notes the systematic eliciting of emotions through the institutions of modern religion, the rise of modern industries of entertainment, and so forth. Expressing his own "disenchantment with [Weber's] Disenchantment [thesis]," Gellner states that late modernity had brought about a con-siderably more flexible "rubber cage" instead (1987): society, increas-ingly, had come to be rationally organized to elicit and mediate *emo-tional* responses. What Gellner shares with other observers is the notion that the human subject, which under early modernity was out-wardly ruled by outcome-oriented, or instrumental, principles, under conditions of late modernity increasingly came to be driven by con-cerns of self-identity and expression of such identity. Being, as de-fined here, became an increasingly organized layer to Doing: Action, increasingly, came to identify Ontology. And the human subject, un-der late modernity, increasingly became involved in reflexively defin-ing its identity. As Anthony Giddens notes (1991, 81; italics added): "In the post-traditional order of modernity, and against the backdrop of new forms of mediated experience, self-identity becomes a *reflex-ively organized endeavor*. The reflexive project of the self, which consists in the sustaining of coherent, yet continuously revised, biographical narratives, takes place in the context of *multiple choice* as filtered through abstract systems. *In modern social life, the notion of lifestyle takes on a particular significance*." Lifestyle, thus understood, refers to the fabric of choices individuals make in daily life. These choices assem-ble as a coherent expression by these individuals of who they are.

What Giddens shares with the otherwise highly divergent thought of French social theorists like Pierre Bourdieu (1984), who looked for cultural expression in consumption choices, Gilles Lipovetsky (1994), who searched for the same in fashion, and German Marxist scholars like Wolfgang Haug (1986), who understood the consumption of material objects to be epiphenomenal of class identity relations, is a focus on choice as a source of identity. For these three theorists, our personal consumption decisions, for example, are guided by our personal narratives of who we are. For some, like Marxist theorists, the narrative link between identity and (material) choice resides outside consciousness and both reflects and determines (that is, reifies) class identity. For others, like theorists following the French social theory of Emile Durkheim and Marcel Mauss, and the German thought of Max Weber and Georg Simmel, the existential consequence of choice is more deliberate and reflective of personal autobiographical narratives. It is this self-referential and self-defining basis to everyday choice—of consumption, of participating in politics through voting, or of anything else—that provides choice with its existential foundation.

Choice as narrative and as motivated by Being is fundamentally different from instrumental choice and Doing as they underlie rational choice theory. To reintroduce the stylized logic of the previous chapter, an instrumentally motivated individual performs an act X solely to create the outcome Y. The value of the act X consequently is determined by its (expected) capacity to bring about Y. Electoral participation, therefore, is paradoxical because of the lack of connection between an individual's vote X and the aggregate electoral outcome Y: if X is not strictly connected to Y, X cannot be of any value to the voter. The paradox resides in the participant nevertheless performing X.

An expressively motivated individual, in contrast, performs X not to generate (or *do*) Y, but *to be* an X-performer and to attach to a collective of (abstractly defined) fellow X-performers. As noted before, the voter votes Democrat not to effect a Democratic electoral victory, but to be a Democrat; consequently, the choice of whether to perform X is determined by what it means to perform X (vote Democrat). The choice of voting, in the expressive context, is an *interpretive* one.

4.1.3 Interpretation and Two Ambiguities

Indeed, the notion of interpretation, together with the notion of ambiguity, is critical to a social theory of expressive choice. Interpretation has taken on relevance along two separate lines for social theorists, one substantive and one methodological. The former focus views humans as inherently interpretive and argues that social science should characterize them in that manner. The latter argues it to be the social theorist's task to pursue an interpretive method. For some scholars the former prescribes the latter. Clifford Geertz, for example, writes: "Believing, with Max Weber, that man is an animal suspended in webs of significance he himself has spun, I take culture to be these webs, and the analysis of it to be . . . an interpretive one in search of meaning" (1973, 5). Others, like Giddens, more explicitly relate interpretive (that is, hermeneutic) methodology and the interpretive nature of the social subject. The emergent complicated relationship between researcher and subject is captured in his terms of "double hermeneutic" and "hermeneutic circle" (Giddens 1982, 1987b). My focus for now remains not with the methodological, but with the substantive application of the term. In this substantive interpretive realm we can begin to answer the second question of this chapter: who are the economic agents in an economy of expressive incentives?

4.1.4 Economic Agents: Producers and Consumers

Interpretively inclined theorists have identified ambiguity as a crucial ingredient to symbolic meaning. Predominantly using the analogy of textual interpretation, participants are seen as "readers," engaged in the act of interpretation.[1] In textual terms, ambiguity defines the distance between the "reader" and his or her "text," and interpretation represents an act of overcoming that distance. Semioticians and, more dramatically, theorists associated with postmodern thought consequently identify the "reader" in this constellation as occupying part of the role of a text's author (Barthes 1988). Reading is a form of assimilation, an act in which images are absorbed and interpreted relative to the reader's cognitive world. Readers are in part authors, precisely because through interpretation they themselves instill a text with meaning. They "make sense" of a text in that they help *manufacture* its sense through their attempts at understanding it.

In hermeneutics, interpretation and understanding occur against a reader's "prejudice," where the term, of course, does not carry its negative colloquial connotations but refers to a framework of preknowledge and prejudgment that determines how a text is understood by its reader (Gadamer 1975, 1976; Skinner 1985). Although hermeneutics and semiotics both find their heritage in the realm of textual interpretation, both are applied to analyses of culture and of

---

[1] "Interpretation" and "Understanding" are equivalent here and are both contained in the Weberian notion of the "sociology of understanding," or *Verstehenssoziologie*.

society. Culture, in hermeneutics, is the shared part of Gadamer's prejudice: it refers to the degree to which individuals' actions are understood in the same way by different members of a collective. Individual action, therefore, is both "social," in that it is embedded in a culturally shared interpretive framework, and "communicative," in that it represents a form of expression within that framework (Habermas 1984–87).

In the context of the economic argument of this book, the single most important difference between hermeneutics on the one hand and neoclassical, or Anglo-Saxon, positivist approaches on the other, is the latter's separation between production and consumption or, in literary terms, between a text's author and its reader. This is crucially relevant to our discussion of consumption benefits.

The neoclassical—and with it the rational choice—image is one of a group of producers creating a good Z for a group of consumers. Producers instill all utility through production, and this utility is realized at the level of consumption: you produce, I consume. You instill value, I take it out. And if you price the good efficiently, I will end up paying a price that corresponds to my utility. In the interpretive context, in contrast, I—like the reader in the textual setting—am involved as Z's coproducer. I participate in instilling value in the product by interpreting it. My voting Republican means something to me, and the source of that meaning, in Gadamer's terms, is partly shared (a cultural understanding of what it means to be voting Republican) and partly personal (my individual interpretation of what it means to be doing so). I, therefore, am in part responsible for manufacturing the symbolic product of Republican voting, of instilling value in the act. Value, consequently, is in part *endogenous* to participation, because *the participant herself instills it through her participation.*

This in itself should prompt us to reconsider radically the role of costs in an expressive context. Recall the example of chapter two, of John Bonaccorso refusing to accept for gratis a front-row seat at Boston's Fourth of July Waterfront Concert. Instead, Bonaccorso preferred to face the steep cost of camping in the park for the entire week prior to the event: "If there's no price, there's no value. . . . I don't want the front unless I earn it." It was precisely because participation entailed a high cost that Bonaccorso was able to establish high expressive value. Because he himself was a coproducer of the value that his participation would generate for him, cost cannot be understood simply as an exogenously imposed hindrance. The modeling of cost in later chapters will therefore formalize the close tying of cost and expressive value.

4.1.5   Ambiguity in Polysemy

I have noted that ambiguity is a crucial aspect of expressive motivation: it invites participants to interpret an activity within the confines of culturally shared understanding, and thus to participate in instilling value in it. There is, however, a second, more direct form of ambiguity, one that occupies a central role for semioticians. It refers to the ability of a symbol to generate a multitude of different meanings, something that anthropologists call "multivocality" (Turner 1967) and semioticians "polysemy" (Eco 1976). If culture is defined as shared meaning, or the extent to which individuals' interpretations overlap, then polysemy defines the variation of different interpretations.

The notion is well illustrated with an example drawn from campaigning. Politicians are notorious for their ambiguity. To invoke a well-known, stylized, and recent example, the Republican National Convention will organize a central message around a term like "family values," whereby the notion is sufficiently ill defined to trigger different associations among different potential participants. Provided the term is kept ambiguous, it is unlikely that there are too many "antifamily" voters that would feel alienated by it. The example is interesting, for it was the Republican party's great misfortune that, in 1992, this ambiguous term was challenged with greatly narrowed and *specific* meaning in the public dialogue that ensued between then vice president Dan Quayle and the situation comedy show *Murphy Brown* (Graber 1997, 188).[2] Rather than leave the term "family values" to resonate with a diversity of demands, it was brought into the specific context of single motherhood. In the pure terms of a product's expressive efficacy, Dan Quayle's error lay not in specifically allowing himself to be seen as critical of single motherhood, but to have any specific opinion on single motherhood come to be associated with him at all. Dan Quayle's error was to restrict the high polysemy of "family values" and force its increased monosemy by applying specific content.

Rational choice and other theorists, too, have focused on the strategic use of ambiguity by candidates. In fact, they have provided two important instrumentally based explanations for why such ambiguity is strategically rational, both of which have some bearing on the expressively based approach being developed here. Both are also incomplete.

[2] The specific example of single motherhood became a salient issue in the 1992 campaign and was carried out in the news media. See, for example, Richard Cohen's "Criticizing Single Mothers" in *The Washington Post*, July 16, 1993, p. 19.

Shepsle (1972) provides a "lottery" account, showing how some voters might hold risk-seeking preferences. These voters prefer a candidate's lottery covering a series of policy positions over his representation of a particular position with certainty. Strategic candidates therefore will be ambiguous about their policy stance because this allows them to secure a large base of electoral support. Page (1976), in contrast, views candidate ambiguity as part of a strategy involving issue salience: in his "emphasis allocation theory" candidates are ambiguous in some policy dimensions in order to emphasize other dimensions selectively. Both theories of ambiguity in essence contain a "spatial" logic: Page views candidate ambiguity as a strategic device to limit issue dimensionality, whereas Shepsle sees it as a device within a particular dimension to overcome the preference heterogeneity of an electorate. In other words, for Page ambiguity is the candidate's device to pick an issue, whereas for Shepsle it is a device to pick a range of stances on that issue. Given their spatial approach to voter choice and for reasons discussed in the previous chapter, both theorists necessarily assume electoral participation.[3]

To some extent, the approaches of Shepsle and Page can be subsumed in an expressively based argument. For voters to be able to attach to candidates for different reasons—in other words, to retain their private meanings of voting for their candidate—requires candidates themselves to remain if not silent, then ambiguous on these reasons. Much like in the instrumental spatial approach, this will involve both a dimensional and a locational aspect. It may be dimensional (as for Page) because voting for the Democratic candidate means different things to different voters. Or it may be a locational concern (thus resembling Shepsle), whereby different voters will associate their preference for, say, fiscal policy with voting for the Democrat, even though their preferences along the fiscal policy dimension are different. In either case, candidates strategically preserve the support of a heterogeneous electorate through ambiguity, as this allows the single act of voting to attract a range of voters.

However, in a much more fundamental way, neither of these instrumental approaches is capable of explaining campaign themes so extremely ambiguous that they convey no substantive information whatsoever. Only if we make the assumption that voters to some extent resonate with expressive or symbolic terms can we regard as strategically rational Ronald Reagan's welcoming "Morning Again in

---

[3] For somewhat more recent treatment, see Enelow and Hinich (1984), chapter seven. As this source shows, our original insights from the original contributions are still relevant.

America" in the early 1980s, George Bush's seeking out "A Thousand Points of Light" in the late 1980s, and Bill Clinton's urging to build a "Bridge to the Twentieth Century" in the 1990s. (In the next chapter I return to these examples in my historical investigation of the rise of expressive campaigning.) These are not merely the product of locational or dimensional spatial strategy, but are instances of *generating* expressive or symbolic essence. In line with the hermeneutic and semiotic arguments, these terms are expressive *because* they are ambiguous. Consequently, there is a dual role for ambiguity in generating expressive motivation. First, if a candidate is successful in generating expressive essence through ambiguity, voters will attach to that candidate and participate in instilling meaning. The act of voting for that candidate, consequently, will have gained symbolic essence. Second, if candidates preserve that ambiguity, then they additionally preserve the ability for different voters to support them for different reasons.

Finally, if expressively focused campaigns rely on ambiguity—first in that ambiguity instills expressive content, and second in that it allows for heterogeneous attachments of voters for different reasons—then we might infer that a strategy of negative campaigning—that is, reducing an opponent's electoral support through attack advertising—involves undercutting the opponent's ambiguity. As campaign history tells us, it was not only *Murphy Brown* that took ambiguity out of the Republicans' family values: Bush and Quayle's Democrat opponents participated in the very same process. I will return to the strategic use of expressively focused negative campaigning in the formal approach of chapter seven.

4.2   OPERATIONALIZING EXPRESSIVE CHOICE

With reference to social theory I have identified three central features to expressive motivation, and each of these provides a theoretical home for different aspects of my investigation of mass participation. I now summarize these features and discuss how the theoretical foundation they provide enables us to operationalize expressive value. Such operationalizing permits me in future chapters to model producers' manipulation of prospective participants' expressive motivation, such as through campaigns in elections designed to elicit greater voter support for a candidate, or through advertising in product markets designed to elicit greater consumption.

First, we have seen that social theorists after Weber have posited a strong motivational human tendency under late modernity toward meaning and expression. This provides a broad theoretical home for expressive motivation and symbolic utility, and for conclusions such as Brennan and Buchanan's, that voters hold "tastes for showing preferences as such."

Second, within that theoretical setting, theorists have identified Choice as an existential source of social identity. Doing, therefore, defines and expresses Being. In chapter two, I stylized the jukebox participant as selecting Sinatra not in order to maximize the likelihood of effecting a desired outcome, but to express to others and to the Self her "Sinatraness." I have made the same argument with respect to voters who vote for the Democratic candidate, in order both to express and to define, in public and in private, their personal "Democratness." In both cases, participation involves the construction of personal identity, the reflexive spinning of what Giddens calls "biographical narratives."

Third, and finally, interpretive social theory has made ambiguity a central component of the interpretive realm. Ambiguity is an unavoidable, indeed necessary, feature to interpretation. My emphasis here, in anticipation of future chapters, has been on noting producers' deliberate manipulation of the participant's motivation via the strategic use of ambiguity in order to generate a multitude of possible reasons why voters might support the candidate.

Yet if we have identified a human tendency toward expressive behavior and acknowledged an existential dimension to such behavior, I have yet to couch these terms in social practice. In other words, if the meaning of action is part shared and part personal, what is it that determines the shared part? Here we can finally embed in theoretical terms some of the dimensions sketched in the jukebox analogy of chapter two.

4.2.1 Expressive Externalities: Butter on the Head

I have emphasized that expressive attachment involves an attachment to a collective—to a "We"—whereby the definition of that collective may be quite vague and will vary among different individuals attaching to the same collective. I have also emphasized that voters in an electoral setting (and, as we shall see in the next chapter, consumers in a market setting) are involved in the instilling of expressive value through interpretation. To characterize these two features in the terminology of political economists, the value of participation is *endogenous* to participation: in the expressive context, it is through the participation of voters and consumers that candidates and goods are given value. The question now is how to operationalize such value.

Anthropologists and social theorists in their work routinely involve two dimensions in establishing an activity's expressive meaning for the individual participant. First, who else is (seen or assumed to be) participating in that activity will determine what it means for the individual to be participating in that activity also, and second, how many others are (seen or assumed to be) participating in the activity will determine what such participation means. Both parameters relate activity (Doing) to identity (Being).

In the realm of electoral participation, the expressive content of voting Democrat will be determined by who else is voting Democrat. If voting Democrat is a defining feature of particular ethnic or occupational groups, and this were known to me, then my own desire to vote Democrat will be affected by this knowledge, as it determines my own understanding of what it means to be a Democratic voter. Second, my understanding of what it means to be a Democratic voter will be determined by the current level of Democratic voting. Belonging to the 20 percent of a population supporting the Democratic ticket, as compared to belonging to a population's 60 percent of Democratic voters, will generate different expressive content for voting Democrat. Although we have yet to explore which of the two settings will be preferable, it is already safe to note that the meaning of participation varies.

The importance of the number and identity of participants in defining an activity's meaning has long been noted by ethnographers, as well as by political scientists who draw on social theory in their work on public opinion. Among the former, for example, the French anthropologist Dan Sperber, observing the ritualistic carrying of butter on the head by members of the Dorze of the Ethiopian highlands remarks: "Butter on the head is only symbolic in so far as it is compared to butter as ordinarily consumed" (Sperber 1975, 53). Analogous to our previous Democratic examples, compare a Dorze society wherein a select few carry butter on the head with one where everybody does, and further compare a society where holders of ritual office carry butter on the head with one where only children do so. The expressive or, in Brennan and Buchanan's (1984) terms, "liturgical" significance of butter carrying is determined by both these parameters.

The expressive logic of Dorze butter carrying is not so far removed from American electoral politics as one might think. Susan Herbst (1993) has demonstrated the importance of quantified information in the form of published opinion polls or surveys in determining citizens' political attachments and political actions. Information concerning the identity and number of individuals is relevant, not only to citizens' political attachment to candidates, but also to citizens' opinion formation more generally. What Herbst calls "numbered voices" reflects how knowledge concerning the "who" and "how many" dimensions, as expressed in public opinion polls, crucially determines individuals' own opinions. More importantly, the very essence of the political landscape, in the account of Herbst and others (e.g., Ginsberg 1989), is defined by individuals' interaction with this type of information. For Dorze butter carriers, for Herbst's opinion holders, as well as for our voters, it is the individual's performance of an action relative to that action's *normal* or *ordinary* use—where these terms themselves are defined by the number and identity of that action's other practitioners—that determines its expressive content.

Stated differently, and in a manner that allows us to apply the language of collective action literature, there is an expressive externality associated with voting and with other forms of participation. The understanding of what it means to be a participant is determined in a collective context, as this understanding changes with every additional visible or anticipated vote. As I will show in the remainder of this book—in the historical illustration of chapter five, and in the analytical approach of chapters six, seven, and eight—this externality allows us to model the economy of expressive incentives in ways akin to how we routinely approach an economy of instrumental, outcome-oriented incentives.

4.3 CONCLUSION

In the previous chapter I reviewed the response to the paradox of participation by theorists who posit moral selective incentives to participation. Reflecting an argument that, earlier, had been made by Democratic theorists, they ask, "What if everybody were thinking selfishly and free-rode on the efforts of others?" There would be an absence of a public good, and the what-if reference to the actions of others addresses the level of *normative principle*.

Then I noted the response to the participation paradox by general equilibrium theorists like Ledyard (1984). Here, too, individuals are concerned with what others are doing, although now this concern does not carry a normative essence, but a *strategic* one: it is precisely in the event that everybody else chooses to free-ride that one's own vote will be decisive. Consequently, it is everybody's recognition of this contingent decisiveness that will once again lead everybody to vote—the cycle continues.

Finally, in the context of expressive choice, there also is a concern among prospective participants with what everybody else is doing. Only now this concern is neither normative nor strategic, but *symbolic*: symbolic value emerges from social practice in that the value associated with an activity itself emerges from what others are seen to be doing.

On the basis of this microfoundation, I provide in the next chapter a history of expressively focused electoral campaigning. I will show how the rise of mass elections in the United States in the twentieth century is well characterized by the development of a strategic manipulation of the *who* and *how many* dimensions through campaigning. As I will also show, this electoral history nicely follows the history of the rise of mass consumer marketing, which, in fact, served as a blueprint to pioneers in expressively focused mass campaigning. Analytically, this electoral history is well understood through reference to economists' and game theorists' notion of "common knowledge." I subsequently formally reconstruct some mass-campaign and -marketing strategies in chapters six through eight.

The economy of expressive choice I analyze in this book is constituted by two types of actors, one expressive and one strategically instrumental. The first are *participants*—voters, interest-group members, consumers. These actors are in essence expressive. The second type of actors are the *producers of participation*—political candidates and their campaigns, interest-group entrepreneurs, marketing experts. These actors are instrumental, yet expressively focused: they strategically target the expressive motivation of prospective participants in order to elicit their participation. They recognize the interpretive relationship between the voter and the election, and that the purpose of campaigning is one of persuasion via a manipulation of *what it means* for the individual prospective participant to be supporting a candidate. The theoretical foundation of this and the previous chapter suggests that the motivational essence of the economy of expressive choice is symbolic, and the manner by which participation is elicited is strategic. The analysis in the next part of this book will focus on the intersection between the two.

PART TWO

ANALYSIS

Chapter Five

SOFT DRINKS AND PRESIDENTS:

THE RISE OF EXPRESSIVE CAMPAIGNS

> The best political commercials are similar to Rorschach
> patterns. They do not tell the viewer anything. They
> surface his feelings and provide a context for him to
> express those feelings.
> *(Tony Schwartz, Eisenhower's media consultant)*

> Would you like to work on this product?
> *(Schwartz being asked to produce
> advertisements for Lyndon Johnson)*

> The reason I liked the Agnew theme was that it didn't
> say anything. You could pick out the reasons why he
> was your kind of man.
> *(Robert Goodman, Agnew's media consultant)*

> Have a Pepsi Day.
> *(Advertising slogan, 1977)*

O N THE BASIS of the theoretical microfoundation established in
the first part of this book, I now provide a summary analytical history of the rise of expressive advertising in both the
product mass market and a in electoral mass campaigning. I show
that producers of participation in both realms faced very similar constraints, with the rise of a mass market and mass electorate respectively, and overcame these constraints by analytically equivalent
means. In fact, as will become evident, political campaign managers
learned from mass marketing experts how to adapt to and master
mass elections.

What emerges in this parallel analytical history is a dimension ignored by economists on the consumption front and by political economists in the context of mass elections. Image-intensive modern mass
advertising and electoral campaigns are institutionalized efforts of af-

fect-intensive *persuasion*. They are not information by which producers and candidates indicate to prospective participants that their product or candidate matches these voters' or consumers' preferences. Campaigns, both in the market and electoral context, are invitations for individuals to attach to a collective of (allegedly existing) participants. In fact, as I will show, with the rising sophistication of mass marketing, producers and campaigns increasingly began to focus on the characteristics of alleged current participants. They did so via the parameters of the *who* and *how many* identified in the previous chapter. Consequently, these efforts at eliciting greater participation encourage an interpretative understanding of voters and consumers of *what it means* to be a participant.

Following the logic of earlier chapters, such campaigning requires the strategic use of ambiguity, both to generate symbolic essence, and to allow for a multitude of different reasons for individual participants to attach. As I will show, this "all-things-for-all-people" approach represents a specific variation of what experts in advertising call "segmented" marketing. In fact, this type of approach, used both in the consumption and electoral contexts, is an integral part of expressive campaigning in both realms.

I begin with an overview of marketing and campaigning, noting that two important purposes of these forms of advertising are, first, to identify a common knowledge dimension among participants and, second, to instill products and candidates (and thereby consumption and voting) with "symbolic essence." I then provide a compressed history of mass marketing in the twentieth century, followed by an equally compressed history of mass campaigning. In both cases I pay particular attention to the producer's strategic manipulation of the expressively important dimensions identified in the previous chapter.

5.1 Marketing and Campaigning

In my approach I include under marketing and campaigning any effort by the producers of participation to manipulate strategically information surrounding a product or candidate in order to elicit greater support among prospective consumers and voters. In addition to forms typically described as "paid media" (that is, of television and print ads), this definition will also include attempts at shaping "free media" through the manipulation of news stories—for example, through efforts known as "spinning" (Scib 1987, 122).

Both the advertising of products in a mass market and of candidates in an electoral campaign represent organized, institutionalized forms of persuasion. Although we may sense some natural resistance to considering these two realms of choice on an equal footing, it is important to acknowledge a shared social and institutional history of advertising and campaign practices. Two historical points in time are crucially important, as they define this common ground. First, in 1948 Rosser Reeves of the Ted Bates Advertising Agency in New York entered the arena of electoral campaigning, culminating in a successful television-led campaign for Eisenhower in 1952. In 1948 Reeves had offered his services to Dewey. However, after shooting a series of trial ads, Dewey rejected them, noting he did not want to be portrayed as a "toothpaste" (Mickelson 1989, 152–54). (Reeves had made his name with the Colgate Palmolive Peet account.) It was the first time that a practitioner of product marketing had offered to enter the world of political campaigning. Thus, as I will show, it is difficult to overestimate the importance of Reeves to the history of electoral campaigning. After Reeves's creation of the Eisenhower ads in the early 1950s, electoral competition in a mass context would never be the same.

If Reeves represents the entry of product advertising techniques into electoral politics, Ronald Reagan's successful bid for reelection in 1984 represents the point at which campaigning achieved full parity with product marketing. Again, Reagan's spots were developed by advertising experts—the "November Group"—rather than by political consultants. But for the first time, they carried the same production value—or "slickness"—as any product counterpart. The very persons who had been involved in the marketing of Pepsi-Cola were now involved in selling a president. Not only do the marketing of soft drinks and the marketing of presidents share a common origin, but to the present day, they share many of the same practitioners.

Although it is fairly straightforward to identify a common history for product and electoral marketing, there is nonetheless no consensus on how advertising generally works—a point noted by some to be an "embarrassment" (Steward 1992, 4). Economists, for the most part, in sharp (and obvious) contrast to researchers in marketing, have paid scant attention to advertising. To the extent that they have, they have seen it as a mechanism for producers to subsidize prospective consumers' search and information costs (Tirole 1988, 289). The purpose of advertising, according to these scholars, is to inform consumers about the qualities of a particular good. With the exception of some Marxists (e.g., Haug 1986), economists have entirely ignored the process of *image* creation, of the producer's indicating to individuals *what it means* to be consuming a particular product. And yet, as the work of marketing historians reveals, the history of advertising involves a systematically increased reliance on such an expressive dimension.

The very same division between advertising-blind economists and marketing scholars is also to be found between political economists modeling electoral behavior and political scientists offering descriptive accounts of campaign practices. The latter group includes scholars like Diamond and Bates (1993), Jamieson (1992, 1996), Sabato (1981), and West (1997). These scholars provide detailed accounts of campaign practices and their often highly emotional content. Political economists, in contrast and in substantive contradiction to these accounts, narrowly tend to see the role of campaigns and advertising as a source of information about candidates and about their policy stances. Again, they pay no attention to the strategic use by candidates and their campaigns of emotionally laden imagery designed to elicit electoral support.

Both in the market case and in the electoral case, these are jarring discontinuities. At the very least by implication, economists on both fronts, unlike their respective marketing counterparts, seem to claim that image does not matter. Yet even a most informal witnessing of advertising and campaign practices indicates an enormous reliance on highly image-intensive political campaign and market advertising practices. As the following historical account will show, an important aspect of the evolution of campaigns and advertising in the twentieth century is an increased shift in focus, away from the product or candidate, to an affect-intensive emphasis of *what it means* for the prospective consumer or voter to participate in consumption or in voting.

On a broader level, this represents an interesting empirical iteration of the theoretical point made by social theorists cited in the previous chapter. I noted an orientation among theorists after Weber to claim a trend, under conditions of "late modernity," toward an increasingly expressive individual. My account of changing marketing and campaign practices in the twentieth century essentially represents an investigation of the institutional dimensions of this trend.[1] Specifically, I show how, first in the product market and subsequently in the electoral market, producers of participation increasingly have come to target prospective participants' expressive desires. In providing this account, I pay particular attention to the relevance of "spatial" models of choice proposed by economists studying consumption choice and by political economists studying voter choice. I will claim that though there were early periods during which product mass marketing and electoral mass campaigning can be shown to have followed a spatial

---

[1] To offer an institutional focus is common for social theorists making a point of cultural-cognitive change. Note, for example, that Weber himself looked for evidence of societal rationalization in the rise of bureaucratic institutions (Weber 1978).

logic, this increasingly has come to be replaced by the very different logic of expressively focused advertising.

5.1.1 Common Knowledge

As I noted in chapter three, a recent trend among political scientists has been to understand the electoral behavior of citizens in a context of "information externalities." For example, an increasing number of scholars look toward poll information as a mechanism by which prospective voters orient their own vote choice, allegedly to avoid "wasting" their vote on candidates unlikely to win (Bartels 1988; Cox 1997; Morton 1991; Alvarez and Nagler 2000). However, as I have already spelled out, the argument works only if voter *choice* is treated in complete isolation from voter *turnout*. The very information that allegedly guides individual citizens' choice of candidates, based on their information concerning other citizens' likely vote intentions, should also indicate to them the extreme irrelevance of their own vote in the outcome of the election. In collective action terms, it is this explicit redundancy that makes electoral participation all the more paradoxical (see chapter three).

There is, however, a similar, yet related and more convincing, "common-knowledge"-based logic applied by some economists, not only to the role of polls and the like, but also to advertising. It is one that is very much in tune with the argument of this book. According to this logic, published information about a product or candidate conveys to individuals two different types of information. First, and most obviously, it conveys information pertaining to the product or candidate. Second, and more important by virtue of its distribution, it conveys the (expressively more relevant) information that everybody else will be receiving this information. Common knowledge implies that everybody knows that everybody knows this information, that everybody knows that everybody knows that everybody knows this information, and so forth. The presence of common knowledge, in contexts like the present, comes not from the informational content provided by an advertisment, but from the common knowledge that is generated by its *distribution*.

A well-suited analogy is that of a flag occupying a town square. Not only do citizens see the flag, but by seeing the flag and observing its location (even if they do so, say, after midnight, when nobody else happens to be around), they see that everybody else sees the flag. To understand the symbolic value of the flag requires that we focus at least in part on individuals' witnessing each other's witnessing the flag. Following the same logic, a citizen receiving information, from news accounts or from campaign statements, about Reagan's alleged standing among voters will know that others, too, are receiving the same information. In a *strictly* expressive context, wherein voters' participation is guided *solely* by an understanding of what it means to be supporting a candidate, this latter dimension will be much more important than the actual manifest informational content.

I noted in the previous chapter that anthropologists consistently identify the *who* and *how many* parameters as determinants of expressive value. The recent application of the common-knowledge literature to advertising represents an analytical extension of that thought. Advertising and campaigning, in this light, are conduits for information pertaining to the collective witnessing of a signal that determines the meaning of one's participation. Such information can be explicit, such as when candidates claim high support levels across a population, or implicit, such as when candidates stress the desirability of being among their supporters, where individual voters will know that all voters receive this message. Our analysis of the evolution of mass appeals through advertising and campaigning, therefore, should involve looking at how producers of participation learn strategically to affect the common-knowledge dimension.

5.1.2 Symbolic Fertility

In the previous chapter I also noted that logically prior to there being a relevance to the *who* and *how many* dimensions, a product or candidate needs to be symbolically "fertile." For the common-knowledge component to matter, advertising must also convey an image that makes expressive attachment attractive to prospective participants. For reasons already discussed, this involves producers' strategic use of ambiguity.

Many scholars studying image-intensive campaigning describe the "feel-good" aspects of candidates as portrayed by their campaigns. For example, Diamond and Bates (1993, 9), describing former astronaut John Glenn's campaign, refer to the "hero symbol who makes us feel good." They and other scholars seek for the same dimension in campaign slogans such as Reagan's "Morning Again in America" and the Ford campaign's song "I'm Feeling Good about America." None of these images provide much, if any, information about policy preferences of candidates. All of them are highly ambiguous.

As the first two opening quotes of this chapter reflect, campaign managers acknowledge their strategic use of ambiguity. Furthermore, in accordance with the theoretical claims of the previous chapter, they explicitly describe ambiguity as a mechanism by which prospective voters are invited to attach expressively to a candidate. Note, for example, how Tony Schwartz, who was Eisenhower's media consultant, states that the purpose of ambiguity is to "surface [viewers'] feelings and to provide a context to *express* those feelings" (see this chapter's opening quotation; cited in Diamond and Bates 1993, 128; italics added). The purpose of campaigning, according to Schwartz, is to provide an expressive context. As I discussed in the previous chapter, prospective voters are thus pulled into the production process as their feelings "surface" in response to the ambiguous campaign ad. Agnews' media consultant Robert Goodman similarly notes how the fact that Agnews' campaign theme "didn't say anything" allowed voters to "pick out reasons" for why they would support him (see this chapter's third opening quotation; Diamond and Bates 1993, 292).

In the previous chapter, I identified two analytical consequences of the use of ambiguity in any attempt at eliciting greater participation. To recap: first, there is an elective affinity between ambiguity and symbolic fertility. For things to be symbolically and thus emotionally meaningful, they must reside on a more ambiguous level. Second, ambiguity keeps candidates dimensionally ambiguous, thus reducing the risk of alienating voters along both expressive-meaning and instrumental-issue dimensions. Again, we don't need to leave the discovery of both these to semioticians, but find them acknowledged by campaign practitioners. Goodman notes in relation to his own use of emotional spots (cited in Diamond and Bates 1993, 311): "most people will agree that voting is a matter of the heart, what you *feel* about someone, rather than a matter of the mind. [The mind] takes what the heart feels, and interprets it. . . . The murky candidate wins. When you get hung up on one side of an issue, there's always a fallout." Goodman's reference to "matters of the heart" matches the notion of symbolic fertility drawn from ambiguity (the first consequence of ambiguity), whereas his warning about getting "hung up on one side of an issue" is in line with the need for dimensional ambiguity (its second purpose). Goodman in some ways makes an even more interesting comment in relation to the need for an emotionally focused strategy when, in relation to Carter's 1976 presidential race, he refers to public opinon polls that "showed that seventy-five percent of the people voting for Carter didn't know his position on one issue—which justifies where I am" (cited in Diamond and Bates 1993, 311).

I have identified several dimensions that are central to the evolution of mass appeals in modern marketing and campaigning. First, I have noted that we must pay attention to a shift by the producers of participation from emphasizing the qualities of their candidate or product to emphasizing *what it means* to be participating in voting for a candidate or consuming a product. This is consistent with what various political scientists have identified as the "consumption dimension" of voting (see chapter three), and I identify this dimension rather literally in this chapter through a comparative focus with product marketing. It also represents what social theorists like Giddens have referred to as the Lifestyle dimension (see chapter four). In this context, it is interesting to note that product advertisers in the early 1950s began switching their efforts to what they themselves called Lifestyle advertising. As we shall see, their definition of the term is fully consistent with my use of it.

Second, I noted that the shift to expressively focused marketing involved incorporating a common-knowledge focus, an emphasis of the *who* and *how many* dimensions of alleged fellow participants. I will demonstrate, as already previewed in the jukebox model of chapter two and developed more carefully toward the end of this chapter, that producers of participation typically emphasize the *how many* dimension, while at the same time often cautiously shielding prospective participants from information concerning the *who*.

Third, and finally, I identified the importance of the strategic use of ambiguity, both to instill products and candidates with symbolic essence, and to keep them ambiguous and allow different participants to attach for different reasons. I introduced the relevant theoretical terms in the previous chapter and have already begun to locate them in the practice of advertising.

With these analytical terms in mind, I now turn to describe the history of mass marketing and campaigning. I begin with a brief history of soft drink marketing in order to show how it foreshadowed the history of presidential campaigning.

5.2 THREE PHASES OF MASS APPEALS: SOFT DRINKS

The business historian Richard Tedlow (1990) identifies three discernible phases in the history of American industrial marketing, and these aptly describe the transformations of the realm of participation, in both the industrial and the electoral spheres. The first phase, a period of *fragmentation*, is one wherein a product (or, by extension, a candidate) is produced locally and wherein, consequently, consumers (and voters) are targeted locally. Soft drinks, in the late nineteenth and early twentieth century, for the most part were put together at local dining establishments, and the primary aim of such soda production was to meet the specific tastes of each of the local customers who occupied the stools lining the soda fountain's counter. The multitude of available refreshments was "compounded by druggists who tried to brighten the day of their customers by concocting new flavors at the soda fountain" (Tedlow 1990, 8–9).

In this local fragmented market, a product's sales volume was low and its price markup high. One beverage, Coca-Cola, was soon to move beyond the boundaries of the local market when, in the early 1890s, Asa G. Candler gained control of the local company. Over the next two decades, Coca-Cola was to be marketed no longer in the "fragmented" setting of the local market, but across a national *mass market*. By 1895 Coca-Cola was available in every state (Cleary 1981). Four years later, Franklin Thomas and Joseph B. Whitehead made a deal with Candler and were granted "the exclusive rights to bottle Coca-Cola within the continental limits of the United States, with the exception of New England, Mississippi, and Texas."[2]

This second *unified* phase involved incorporating the entire nation in a single mass market. In the unified mass market a product's sales volume is high and its markup margin decreased dramatically, even more so with the introduction of competitors. The transition to the unified mass market was enabled by technological development. Coca-Cola first entered the mass market at a time during which the country saw the emergence of a solid railroad and telegraph network. Drastically lower transportation costs, coupled with the fact that soft drinks could be distributed through a bottler network largely reliant on independent franchises, enabled the producer's entry into a mass market. This was the rise of the powerful brand: "they wanted everyone to drink it anytime, as their advertising stressed. To achieve this goal, they launched a coordinated advertising and sales force drive so well executed that it created one of the most powerful brands in the history of marketing" (Tedlow 1990, 22).

In the unified market, large industrial producers created one product with the aim of capturing the varied tastes of a maximum number of potential consumers. To do so, following "spatial" logic, they targeted a median preference of the population of prospective consumers. Here Coca-Cola was first known to embark on its quest for the "universal cola" (much like Henry Ford, famously, had told his prospective customers that they could have their car any color they wanted, "as long as it was black"). In terms of advertising, Coca-Cola followed its median-preference targeting by producing taste-focused ads (*Beverage World*, Fall 1993, 132–48). Among the best-known slogans of that period were "Drink Coca-Cola, Delicious and Refresh-

---

[2] Thomas's operation continued until 1975, when the Coca-Cola company regained its bottling contract rights for approximately $35 million.

ing" (1904), "It's Clean and Pure, That's Sure" (1909), and "The Best Drink Anyone Can Buy" (1913).

Coca-Cola's market strategy came to another transition in the late 1940s and early 1950s when its main competitor, Pepsi-Cola, could no longer pursue a strategy of underpricing, as it had done in previous years. Pepsi, suddenly, found itself needing to invent a new marketing approach in order to survive the increasingly hostile Cola wars: for the first time in the history of soft drink marketing, a producer systematically devised a strategy that targeted consumers according to *their* identity characteristics. As Tedlow notes (1990, 23), it was the first time that a producer enhanced consumption "by appealing to customers on the basis of who they were rather than what the product was." This would give rise to ambiguous identity-focused terms like the "Pepsi Generation" (1960), and Coke's imperative to "*be* sociable" (1955). This was the beginning of the *segmented* phase—the emergence of a marketing approach that would revolve around demo- and "psychographics." In two different senses, the segmented phase of mass marketing shares characteristics with both the fragmented and unified phases. Like the fragmented phase, market segmentation involved customizing the product to fit the different needs of prospective consumers. Like the unified phase, market segmentation involved a mass market selling a product at high volume with low markup pricing.

There are in fact two important ways in which producers segmented the mass market. First, and most obvious, they attempted to capture varied tastes by manufacturing a host of line extensions, whereas previously they had offered a single product (Tirole 1988, 281–82; Scherer and Ross 1990, 600–10). "Supermarket shelves are so crowded with line extensions. The world of the universal cola—the one brand perfect for anyone, anytime, anywhere—is now gone" (Tedlow 1990, 230). The original single product had been joined by several others (like Diet Coke, Cherry Coke, Caffeine-Free Coke, and Caffeine-Free Diet Coke), as well as noncola drinks produced by the Coca-Cola company (including Tab, Sprite, Diet Sprite, Caffeine-Free Tab, Fresco, Fanta, and, of course, Mello Yello).

A second, even more interesting, type of segmentation is to be found in the use of ambiguous images and has already been identified in the context of electoral campaigning: what are the campaign strategies noted in the comments of Schwartz and Goodman, with respect to Rorschach patterns and voters picking out their own reasons for supporting a particular candidate, but forms of market segmentation? As with market segmentation, different prospective participants are provided an opportunity to attach to "different" candidates or products for different reasons. Market segmentation through ambiguity will always be more efficient than the use of line extensions. In both the product and context the electoral context, the variation of tastes and preferences among a mass audience of prospective participants will always exceed the variety of products that one producer can supply. This is particularly pertinent in the mass-electoral context, wherein one single candidate is expected to bridge the distribution of preferences among a very large number of voters.[3] In addition, the use of such ambiguity not only allows a better bridging of a wide variety of preferences, but also invites attachment in the first place. In collective action terms, it will mobilize participants. For both choice and turnout reasons, therefore, segmentation through ambiguity should represent a more powerful strategy with respect to enhancing a product's or candidate's market or electoral support. I will demonstrate this point formally in chapter seven.

5.2.1 From Price- to Lifestyle-Focused Competition

It is important that the history of Coca-Cola be understood in a competitive context. Not only was much of Coca-Cola's advertising strategy formulated in response to Pepsi-Cola's threat, but Pepsi itself had come to invent much of what became expressively focused advertising. More interesting still, we can learn from two types of failures that Pepsi experienced in its attempts at competing in a mass market— one using instrumentally focused price-based advertising, and one reversing its course of Lifestyle-based advertising.

The original Pepsi-Cola recipe was invented by Caleb Bradman in 1898—thirteen years after John Pemberton had invented Coca-Cola, and a year before the rights to Coca-Cola's national franchise bottling was sold. By 1910 Coca-Cola had established 370 bottlers nationwide, whereas Pepsi had established 280 in 24 states. In the early decades, Pepsi competed on the basis of price. Its famous early slogan was "Twice as Much for Half the Price." However, with the dramatically rising price of sugar in the 1920s, the company was forced to raise its price, losing a great deal of market volume, and faced bankruptcy in the process.

It recovered. However, twenty years later, in the mid-1940s, Pepsi-Cola again faced bankruptcy, allegedly "hurt by [its] product's bargain image" (Muris, Scheffman, and Spiller 1993, 39). Finally, in 1950, a year during which Pepsi's earnings had fallen 78 percent, Alfred

---

[3] As I will address in greater detail in this chapter, early mass campaigning did in fact involve a single candidate presenting himself very differently to different prospective constituencies.

Steele, a former vice president of Coca-Cola, took over at Pepsi-Cola. As reported in the *New York Times* on February 7, 1956, Steele took the company's marketing efforts from price advertising to image-based advertising, beginning with the introduction of a new bottle and the Lifestyle-focused advertising campaign "Be Sociable—Enjoy the Light Refreshment." Steele's wife, actress Joan Crawford, certainly helped the glamorous image of the product and toured as a speaker at bottlers' meetings. Between 1950 and 1958, Pepsi revenues increased over 300 percent, and its ratio of Coke-to-Pepsi sales decreased to 2.5 to 1 (Muris, Scheffman, and Spiller 1993, 40).

In the very beginning of the 1960s, Pepsi introduced the notion of a Pepsi "generation." It began with "Now It's Pepsi—for Those Who Think Young," noting in its copy that the Pepsi generation "includes everyone with a young view of things." From 1962 to 1967 the company used the slogan "Come Alive! You're in the Pepsi Generation!" In a literal, explicitly "demographic," way, the company stressed an identity that would be expressed as the product was consumed. Interestingly, it had also kept the demographic identifier extremely ambiguous, to entice as many prospective consumers as possible. According to Alvin Pottash, senior vice president of creative services in 1980, the Pepsi Generation was calculatedly very large (stressing a high *how many* dimension). He noted that the label referred to a "special breed of people, not an age-group". Indeed, a survey at the time showed that 62 percent of men and women between the ages of thirteen and twenty-four identified themselves as belonging to the "Pepsi Generation," but so did 43 percent of those aged thirty-five to forty-nine (Forkan 1980, 43).

In the mid-1960s Pepsi executives made a very instructive strategic error. They abandoned the highly successful, expressive Lifestyle focus that they had introduced in the mid-1950s, and had developed throughout the early 1960s, when in 1966 they went back to building their advertising around a product focus. Following an early unified marketing theme, they produced the slogan "The Taste That Beats the Others Cold. Pepsi Pours It On." The campaign was a great failure, and Pepsi's market share decreased rapidly. Soon thereafter, the Pepsi Generation theme was revived with "You've Got a Lot to Live. Pepsi's Got a Lot to Give," which was used until 1973. In 1977 consumers were invited to "Have a Pepsi Day."

From this compressed marketing history we learn that producers initially responded to the challenge of facing a mass market of prospective consumers with diverse tastes by aiming for the most widely liked, median taste and by promoting this explicit effort through advertising. With the introduction of competitors, the market became increasingly constrained to the extent that it could be captured on the basis of a product's qualities alone. The logic at work is a spatial one: a population's preference spectrum is divided among producers, and the larger the number of producers in the market, the smaller the maximum number of consumers they can capture on the dimension of taste alone (Hotelling 1990; Downs 1957; Shepsle 1972). In addition, as we see from Pepsi's early attempts at breaking into the mass market, which twice nearly rendered the company bankrupt, price-focused marketing of a product makes demand for the product highly elastic, that is, price sensitive. (I will illustrate this aspect formally in chapter seven, where I look at the trade-off between instrumentally and expressively focused campaigning.)

The introduction of Lifestyle-centered marketing shifts the focus of advertising away from the product to what its consumption reflects of a consumer's Lifestyle, of who she is. In the terms established in the previous chapter, the product is offered by the producer to be included in consumers' "biographical narratives." Advertising becomes increasingly ambiguous, and increasingly references are made to Lifestyle consequences by suggesting the product's popularity among *many*, while also allowing individual consumers themselves to associate with its consumption a variety of *who*'s. In terms of our theoretical distinction, Lifestyle advertising represents a strategic shift in focus toward a prospective consumer's *Being*.

5.3 THREE PHASES OF MASS APPEALS: PRESIDENTS

I now identify in presidential campaigning a progression through the same three phases identified in mass marketing. I begin with the *fragmented* phase in the era of the whistle-stop, proceed with the median-preference-seeking *unified* phase emerging with the rise of early mass media, and end with the expressively focused, television-led *segmented* phase of modern image-intensive campaigning.

5.3.1 "Whistle-stop" Fragmentation

Prior to the twentieth century, presidential candidates did very little on-the-road campaigning. William McKinley, in 1896, mostly sat on the front porch of his home in Canton, Ohio, and voters went to see him (Scib 1987, 124). This changed with the era of whistle-stop campaigning: "The train stopped on sidings and in freight yards of towns, both large and small. Advance men were charged with delivering an enthusiastic crowd supported by bands, cheerleaders, pom-pom girls, and local dignitaries, all assembled alongside the tracks. When the whistle blew, the crowd knew the train was approaching and would soon stop. So, they stood awaiting the 'whistle-stop'" (Mickelson 1989, 98).

Whistle-stop campaigning, like early fragmented marketing, involved approaching different localities and, thus, different audiences separately. Voters were addressed at different times without the overarching presence of the electronic media. Even audiotape recording, in these early days, was too cumbersome to have any practical value in the field: this was the "era of the purely verbal report" in which a news item, effectively, was a "think piece, delivered by the correspondent" (Mickelson 1989, 98). While members of the printed media traveled along with the campaign, candidates could vary their claims to meet local preferences, provided this did not result in stark factual contradictions. For example, farmers' concerns were typically at odds with those of urban populations, and successful politicians were capable of switching not only themes and promises, but also performance styles to suit the venues in which they appeared. In market terms, the presidential campaign was able to provide a variety of products to meet different consumers' tastes. And although, ultimately, such campaigns attempted to appeal to an entire nation of voters, they had to do so while approaching the population by means of independent fragments. Political campaigns, in the fragmented phase, lacked the means to target audiences much beyond one locality at a time.

This resembles the early small-scale soda-fountain scenario, where many different soda-fountain-sized markets used the same base syrup to produce a variety of concoctions for their customers. And just as these concoctions were adapted to suit each individual consumer's preferences, one and the same candidate would portray different versions of himself in a manner thought to appeal most to audiences of each venue.

5.3.2 Median Preference Unification

The rise of radio signaled the beginning of the end of fragmented electoral campaigning. In 1924 Democrat John W. Davis and Republican Calvin Coolidge both purchased radio airtime for speeches. The Democrats spent forty thousand dollars on broadcast time, whereas the (victorious) Republicans spent three times as much. That year about 3 million households had radios. Exactly ten years later ten times as many, or 30 million households, did (Scib 1987, 124).

On August 8, 1928, the *New York Times* commented on how the advent of radio had a strong impact on the campaign styles of politicians (cited in Jamieson 1996, 20): "Radio 'hook-up' has destroyed the old-time politicians' game of promising in each locality the things which that locality wishes. They can no longer promise the Western farmer higher prices for wheat without arising the Eastern factory population against higher bread prices." The rise of a new, overarching communication structure put an end to purely fragmented campaigning and signaled the beginnings of a unified electorate market. This rise was gradual, as radio broadcasts had yet to gain nationwide reach. But even prior to technology allowing for this kind of scope, political campaigns already attempted to address the country as a unified electorate. For example, in the same year that the *Times* made its comments, the GOP organized six thousand "Minute Men" across the nation to read brief radio speeches for the Republican candidacy. These men were sent scripts in advance, so that each of them would give the same talk on the same day. Even though they still lacked sophisticated technological means, political campaigns were already devising means to market candidates in a "national" manner.

Because of its increasingly unified focus, campaigns now sought to focus on themes that would appeal to the largest number of prospective voters, rather than to approach independent fragments with different themes. For example, Harry Truman's campaign produced a dramatization in which an "average housewife" complained about rising food prices, holding the Republican Congress responsible. Eisenhower's early campaigns in the 1950s focused on national security. Like early unified Coca-Cola marketing, these campaigns chose substantive themes that would be expected to match the policy concerns of a maximum number of voters.

5.3.3 Expressive Segmentation

Beginning in the 1950s, political campaigning again began to change with the rise of television, and with it began the decade that would slowly usher in expressively focused campaigning. That year 9 percent of American households had television, and over the subsequent five years this figure rose to 65 percent (Scib 1987, 126). Rosser Reeves of the Ted Bates Advertising Agency in New York had approached Dewey in 1948 to produce television ads for his campaign. After viewing some initial spots produced, Dewey rejected this approach because of its "toothpaste" quality, noting that TV advertising would not be "dignified" enough for a presidential campaign (Mickelson 1989, 152; Diamond and Bates 1993, 41). Dewey reacted both to the product-feel of the sample ads filmed (but never broadcast), as well as to Reeves's well-known product advertising background, which included designing a Colgate Palmolive campaign, as well as inventing the well-known M&M's chocolate slogan "Melt in Your Mouth . . . Not in Your Hands."

Four years later, in 1952, the Eisenhower team employed Reeves to produce a series of campaign ads for its presidential campaign. Reeves produced the well-known "Eisenhower Answers America" spots: these featured the candidate answering questions allegedly posed by ordinary citizens. (The citizens, in fact, were people picked as they were waiting in line for an entirely unrelated event in New York. They spoke their questions only after Eisenhower's answers had already been taped.) In some ways, Eisenhower's campaign ads followed the strategy of unified marketing: they targeted issues found to be representative of widely held preferences. In more important ways, however, this advertising offered a "glimpse" into the future (Sabato 1981, 111), of what expressively focused campaigning would be like.[4] The ads pictured not just the candidate, but his supporters, who were "ordinary" citizens. The ads also increasingly became affect intensive as they began to involve "feel-good" imagery. This was the beginning of expressive campaigning.

Another indication that Eisenhower's campaign represented a transition toward the segmented phase was his strategic use of ambiguity. Such ambiguity, however, involved specific policy issues, rather than an avoidance of such issues. In that sense, the campaign was still caught up in a fragmented approach, trying to be all things to all people. Only now, unlike in the fragmented setting, all people were watching at the same time. Jamieson describes this substantive ambiguity:

> On cue Ike played either Santa or Scrooge. He appeared as all things to all people. In a move comparable to that of Carter in '76 and Reagan in '80, the general promised to increase services and decrease taxes by cutting out fraud, waste, and corruption. He pledged to "put a lid on government spending" in one ad but promised "expanded Social Security and more real benefits" in another, more tanks and planes for Korea in a third, and a cut in taxes in a fourth. Democratic ads highlighted Ike's "promise them anything" posture by stating that Stevenson "is too honest to promise drastic cuts and adequate preparedness at the same time" (1996, 84).

Eisenhower's running mate, Richard Nixon, displayed an equally inconsistent approach. And like Eisenhower, Nixon had begun to couch this inconsistency in symbol-intensive terms. A most striking

[4] Scib (1987, 125–56) makes a similar point as he notes that the first television advertising "of consequence" appeared during the 1952 presidential race, although 1960 marked the "real power of television."

example of this is to be found in Nixon's infamous "Checkers" speech. Upon revelation that Nixon had inappropriately drawn on a fund to pay his personal expenses, calls for his resignation from the Republican ticket emerged. In response, in an emotional and distracting speech that reached 48.9 percent of the possible television audience (Jamieson 1996, 71), Nixon offered to return everything deemed inappropriately received, except for a little dog—Checkers—that had been shipped in a crate and that had elicited the love of Nixon's kids. With respect to the allegations made against Nixon's use of funds, the speech was filled with irrelevancies (including the dog), obvious lies, and obvious inconsistencies. Yet it resulted in 2 million telegrams, letters, and phone calls making their way to the Republican National Committee, allegedly showing support for Nixon on the ticket at a ratio of 350 to 1 (Jamieson 1996, 77).

Both Nixon and Eisenhower had begun to learn to use emotion in television to elicit a mass electorate's attachment. And this affect intensity seemed to ameliorate their inconsistencies. The Eisenhower-Nixon half of the 1952 campaign represents the early beginnings of expressively focused campaigning, brought into play under the guidance of a product marketing expert. It involved an early, rudimentary use of symbolically fertile imagery and introduced an equally rudimentary emphasis on how attractive it was to be an Eisenhower-Nixon supporter. At the same time, their inconsistencies provided a variety of accounts that could meet the competing demands of different prospective constituencies. If Goodman is right, that voting is a "matter of the heart" and that the "mind takes what the heart feels and interprets it," then Eisenhower's multitude of inconsistent policy promises, as well as Nixon's multitude of internally inconsistent explanations concerning his illegitimate use of funds, are instances of offering voters a variety of ways in which they could justify, to themselves and to others, why they supported either or both these candidates. To use Goodman's language, which draws on Spiro's campaign theme, voters could simply "pick out" reasons why either candidate was "their kind of man." Segmentation, in this form, did not resemble soft drink producers' creation of line extensions, but their use of ambiguity in order to generate many different reasons for prospective participants to attach. Meanwhile, throughout the campaign Eisenhower's opponent, Stevenson, preferred to continue giving simple policy-focused speeches, complaining all the while about the "compressing force of television," and about Eisenhower's "*all-things-to-all-men* demagoguery" (cited in Jamieson 1996, 104).

If Eisenhower began the segmented phase in the 1950s, the Kennedy campaign took it further in 1960 and 1964. In 1960 the campaign gave its ads the look of short documentaries and increasingly showed images of current (alleged) supporters. For example, while Kennedy was shown speaking to coal miners, the camera would pan across their faces, covered in grime. That year, and more so in 1964, the Kennedy campaign also became increasingly emotional and symbol intensive. While both of these strategies had already been employed by Eisenhower, Kennedy's ads were considerably slicker and made these earlier attempts appear stilted. Furthermore, unlike Eisenhower, Kennedy refrained from making many inconsistent claims. Instead, he anchored his ambiguity at the image level.

To the present day, presidential campaigns involve the use of highly ambiguous, symbolically fertile feel-good imagery. Examples abound. A very literal one is to be found in 1976, Gerald Ford's use of the song "I'm Feeling Good about America; I'm Feeling Good about Me." Ronald Reagan in 1980 referred to the late John Wayne, who "did not believe our country was ready for the dustbin of history," and in 1984 stressed that it was "Morning Again in America." George Bush saw "A Thousand Points of Light," and Bill Clinton proposed his vision of "Building a Bridge to the twenty-first Century."

At the same time, campaigns increasingly targeted the *what it means* dimension by focusing not on the candidate, but on his supporters. Eisenhower had begun to do this in the 1950s, and Kennedy had done it in the 1960s; Nixon ads in 1968 did not even show Nixon, and Reagan's original "Morning in America" ads did not show Reagan. All ads, however, indicated a mass of supporters, either implicitly (as in Reagan's depiction of rolling hills and picket-fence towns across America), or explicitly, like Bush's 1980 primaries ads featuring what Diamond and Bates characterize as "big crowds and miniscule information" (1993, 251).

5.4   Shielding: The "Lennons" Problem

I have noted in the previous chapter the importance of the *who* dimension, in addition to the *how many*, in determining the expressive value of attaching to a candidate through one's support. This takes us back to a common-knowledge argument. Just as candidates could quickly become attractive to voters by being identified with a type of alleged supporter, they could also be made to be very unattractive through association with highly unappealing supporters. An extreme form is to be found in anti-Goldwater campaigning. The most negative ads in 1964 depicted the Ku Klux Klan burning crosses and quoted a Klan official as saying, "In Alabama, we hate niggerism,

Catholicism, and Judaism. . . . I like Barry Goldwater. He needs our help" (Diamond and Bates 1993, 132; Scib 1987, 130).

Following common-knowledge logic, the potential power of such ads comes not from how credible their information is—in this case identifying Goldwater as Ku Klux Klanian in his policies. Instead, it comes from the common knowledge that a suddenly publicly available interpretation for being a Goldwater supporter is to belong to a collective that includes the Ku Klux Klan. These ads provided less information about Goldwater, but instead contested citizens' understandings of what it meant to support Goldwater. As I will explore in the formal context of chapter eight, associating candidates with particular supporters continues to be a powerful tool in negative campaigning. Note, for example, the emphasis of David Duke's alleged association with the KKK in 1990. Regardless of the accuracy of this claim, for voters, supporting Duke now potentially represents an association with a collective that includes the KKK. This is yet another extreme example. On a much milder front, note presidential candidate Bob Dole's association with then highly unpopular Newt Gingrich in 1996, and how this association was widely believed to narrow his support (West 1997, 5).

While producers strategically provide us with a great deal of information about how many others are allegedly partaking in a participatory good X, they also typically invest a fair amount of effort shielding potential participants from the characteristics of other participants. This pattern holds true for a remarkable variety of instances of mass participation. In chapter two, I compared the diverse examples of customers making selections on a café jukebox; the consumption of theater, cinema, and concert products; and the pattern of restaurant seating arrangements, noting how in all cases, participants are actively made aware of the large number of alleged fellow participants, but at the same time are shielded from learning who, specifically, these others are. I also noted how political candidates typically make reference to their vast numbers of supporters while at the same time concealing the characteristics of those alleged supporters. In all these cases, producers appear to assume that knowledge of *who* else is participating in a good X is potentially a liability.

As I noted throughout part one, the identity of fellow participants matters greatly in determining the meaning of a participatory good X. A striking example in the private-good industrial case—one after which I name this phenomenon[5]—is found in the music industry and its notable absence of company-sponsored "fan" clubs. This example

[5] With apologies to Akerlof (1984).

provides a nice summary for the logic of shielding in the context of mass participation. Where one might expect record companies to encourage such organized consumption, they instead undermine it, or at least very stringently control any third-party fan organizations.[6] To apply one stylized example, the product of John Lennon can be characterized as both a "yuppie" and a "hippie" phenomenon. Consequently, to have such different types of consumers confront each other in one and the same fan club will affect the identity definition of what it means, to individual participants, to attach themselves to the product of John Lennon: I, a yuppie, will begin to read Lennon very differently when I see you, a hippie, also consuming Lennon. Seeing you being a Lennon consumer will affect what I believe to be the significance of consuming Lennon. My *yuppie-specific* utility of consuming John Lennon, consequently, will drop.

As with the jukebox producer in chapter two, the successful Lennon producer, in this light, faces the task of stressing the existence of a large number of Lennon participants, while at the same time screening individual participants from the specific identity characteristics of fellow participants. The producer may even stress that everyone consumes Lennon, yuppies and hippies included, thereby allowing the participant (yuppie or hippie) to attach herself to the global collective of Lennon participants. At the same time, such attachment is an abstract one and does not contradict the fact that firsthand observation of fellow participants' participation (such as in a fan club) will reduce the interpretive scope of the participatory good. As with the jukebox, the practice of stressing numbers allows the individual participant to attach expressively to a collective by participating in X. The practice of shielding allows a multitude of different attachments to occur and prevents the consumer from being discouraged by any specific identification with any actual members of that collective.

In the semiotic terms noted in chapter four, this can be understood as a producer's strategy of preserving polysemy, or multivocality. Campaign managers frequently display their candidates in front of large, yet anonymous, mass audiences. Candidate George Bush's campaign in 1992 made great effort to minimize in front of the general public the endorsement of voters associated with the National Rifle Association. Jesse Jackson, in 1988, refused endorsement by several gay rights groups. Similarly, Pepsi-Cola's television advertisements display large groups of consumers applying lighting resembling the dark and anonymous mass audiences of pop concerts. Coca-Cola commercials, more extremely, avoid personal identity characteristics altogether by having their product consumed by animated

---

[6] This illustration relies on fieldwork conducted in Britain in 1988–89.

polar bears. In all cases, the vast mass of participants is stressed (even polar bears drink it!). Yet in all cases, the prospective participant witnesses the collective only via its silhouette.

5.5 CONCLUSION

We saw that the history of marketing and campaigning is the evolution of an approach by producers to be all-things-to-all-people. In the technologically most limited phase—the fragmented phase—products and candidates were most literally so, as producers sought out each participant's (or, in the electoral case, each group of participants') preferences in order to meet them. The purpose of advertising was simply to indicate the relevant qualities of the good, or of the candidate.

In the unified phase, products and candidates had to become single things that most people would like. An advantage here, due to technological innovation, was that the producers' reach was tremendously greater. A disadvantage was that producers could no longer deal with preference diversity. This period of marketing and campaigning, therefore, comes closest to displaying the logic proposed by spatial theorists whereby producers position themselves along prospective participants' preference spectrums in order to capture the support of the majority. The choice of position, in this effort, is determined both by the distribution of preferences among consumers and voters, as well as by the strategic positioning of competing producers. In addition, prospective participants choose along a low-affect, instrumental dimension.

The end of the unified phase came when producers returned to an all-things-to-all-people strategy. Only now they did so in the mass market, rather than in the fragmented market. Initially, they did so with line extensions—literally so in the product market, and by offering many competing policy-focused promises in the electoral campaign. In the latter context, candidates—specifically Eisenhower and Nixon—learned that such inconsistencies could be managed better in connection with a symbol-intensive, expressive-attachment-inviting approach. More sophisticated versions, beginning with Kennedy and achieving their height since Reagan in 1984, involved not an ambiguity that would incorporate the selling of a multitude of policy positions, but a *replacement* of policy positions by an ambiguity that would invite expressive attachment.[7]

---

[7] I was once told by a car salesman (*after* I had bought my car) that the trick is to have a customer fall in love with the car on the showroom floor. Then just provide

If electoral campaigning has followed the footsteps of product marketing across the century, an emerging question is, What can be learned about electoral campaigning in the future by looking at product marketing now?

Two speculations come to mind. First, with the proliferation of customized information channels via cable television and Internet distribution, the potential for providing demographically and psychographically targeted narrowcast information is tremendous. At the same time, such customized information delivery loses its crucially important common-knowledge dimension: recipients can no longer believe that they are witnessing a public event (that is, implicitly witnessing others' witnessing, or being witnessed by that witnessing) as they receive such information. Consequently, the most potent feature for mass advertising and campaigning appears to involve the use of a two-tier, simultaneous narrow- and broadcasting strategy. Such would provide specific product or candidate information via customized channels, while at the same time allowing this tailored information to resonate with the ambiguous, symbol-intensive portrayal of the product or candidate in the explicitly public realm. On informal observation, this appears to be a strategy gradually emerging in the product market, and there is enormous potential for it in electoral campaigning.

A second speculation concerns the use of public endorsement of products and of candidates by celebrities or other individuals. Apparently for "Lennons"-problem reasons, product advertisers have decreased the use of celebrity spokespeople over time, and for the same reason we ought to expect a similar decrease of public endorsements in the realm of expressively focused political campaigning. Although widely publicized endorsements might be expected to help launch a product or a candidate (that is, gain them acceptance among a significant portion of the population), beyond a particular level, such endorsement should become a constraint. This is identical to the constraints of the *who* dimension, wherein familiarity with the specific characteristics of actual participants will reduce the interpretive scope of what it means to be a participant oneself. If advertisements in the beginning of the expressive-segmented phase have begun to shift

---

"very mild assistance" as the consumer starts assembling his or her own list of technical (rational) reasons why the car ought to be the right choice. This is a version of participants being drawn into the production process, as noted in theoretical terms in chapter four, and as applies to the offering of a diversity of invitations for electoral attachment here. On a related note, Ernest Gellner in his lectures would describe Hume's notion of rationality with the summary sentence "Reason is the aftertaste of emotion."

much of their attention away from the candidate to the alleged participant, the next step is to shift this emphasis again, away from the participant to some more ambiguous reference to the types of people who participate. In many areas, this already has begun to happen—again see Coca-Cola's choosing to show polar bears instead of human faces, and Ronald Reagan's "Morning in America" ads showing people's homes and a rolling countryside, rather than showing people.

In the remaining three chapters I pursue by simple formal means some of the campaign strategies noted here. In chapter six, I formalize instrumental and expressive returns to participation and show how the presence of expressive returns will result in participatory bandwagons. These will arise in both the product and the electoral settings, and all that is required is that only some of the participants be driven by expressive desires. The model offers a microlevel approach that generates the type of aggregate-level momentum observed by political scientists studying elections.

In chapter seven I show that instrumentally focused campaign strategy not only necessarily will be insufficient for voters to overcome the collective action problem, but will in fact diminish the effectiveness of an expressive campaign. This is the formal version of the argument that the Pepsi-Cola company twice nearly went under because it tried to appeal to consumers on the basis of price. Equivalently, and in stark contrast to the reality portrayed in spatial models of voter choice, presidential candidates would not stand a chance in an election today if they were to compete on issue dimensions alone. I call the trade-off between instrumental ($+$) and expressive ($-$) utility in these settings "expressive crowding out." In that analytical context I can also show that for expressive reasons, negative campaigning will result in the "shrinking and polarization of an electorate," as observed by Ansolabehere and Iyengar (1995). Finally, I relate these analytical findings to the social theory surrounding the term "commodification."

In chapter eight I show how expressively campaigning producers compete by generating electoral momentum among the population. Using simple tools from price-theory microeconomics, I incorporate the cost constraints of producing participation this way and show how such campaigning affects the composition of participants' utility.

Chapter Six

EXPRESSIVE UTILITY AND MOMENTUM

You Like Ike, I Like Ike, Everybody Likes Ike!
(Advertising slogan)

IN CHAPTERS three and four I sought out a social-theoretical justification and foundation for expressive choice. In chapter five, on
the basis of this foundation, I provided a historical account of how
producers of participation in both the mass-electoral and mass-market
realm strategically came to elicit participation by targeting prospective participants' expressive motivation. In this chapter I introduce a
simple formalization of a theoretical microfoundation, so that in the
next two chapters I can model some aspects of the expressively focused campaigning and marketing practices I identified in the historical account. Throughout the remainder of this book, I will keep the
level of formalization low.[1]

After introducing and refining a basic model, and generating predictions involving momentum in expressively motivated electoral and
market participation, I discuss the relevant literature on bandwagons
and bandwagon preferences. I show how the present analysis at the
microlevel provides an explanation for momentum that sidesteps the
internal inconsistencies of the instrumentally based explanations I
mentioned in chapter three. I further note how this analysis also provides detailed contours to the symbolically or expressively based explanations provided by theorists like Herbst (1993) and Edelman
(1988). I close the chapter with a formal statement of the strategic
interests of producers of mass participation in market and electoral
arenas.

---

[1] Although the first part of the model will involve the use of some simple equations,
the remainder of the analysis in this and future chapters will almost exclusively rely on
graphical representation. Readers may want to browse quickly through the opening
section of this chapter until they reach section 6.1.3, at which point the analysis becomes graphically based and assumes no familiarity with formal expression.

6.1 THE MODEL

The i-th individual's utility for candidate X is determined by an expressive and an instrumental component:

$$u_i^x(n_x, q_i^x) = \underbrace{f_x(n_x)}_{\text{expressive}} + \underbrace{q_i^x}_{\text{instrumental}} \tag{6.1}$$

In this simple form, the expressive component to the participant's utility is captured in the very general expression $f_x(n_x)$, which states that the number of X-participants determines the value the individual X-participant derives out of her participation in X.[2] The instrumental component of the utility function is denoted by q_i^x. I begin my discussion here.

6.1.1 Instrumental Returns to Participation

As noted in chapter three, the instrumental return associated with voting for X, q_i^x, is determined by two factors. First, it is driven by an individual voter's preference of one candidate over the other. Second, it is determined by the voter's calculation of the expected impact of her vote on the result of the election. Following the instrumental-returns-to-participation model introduced in chapter three, an expression for q_i^x is:

$$q_i^x = pB_i^x - C_i \tag{6.2}$$

where p denotes the probability of determining the result of the election with a single vote; B_i^x denotes a contingent benefit that is realized if, indeed, the individual's vote determines the outcome of the election; and C_i is voter i's cost of participation in the election, expressed in utility terms.

This equation is equivalent to the standard returns-to-voting expression proposed in collective action approaches to voter *turnout* (see section 3.1). Following spatial approaches to voter *choice*, I now expand the expression to show how the magnitude of B_i^x in this cal-

---

[2] As discussed in chapters four and five, expressive value is a function of the number and the identity of fellow participants. Since producers of large-scale participation generally shield the *who* dimension while manipulating the *how many* dimension, I begin my formalization with a focus on the role of the number of X-participants. In chapter eight I additionally investigate how the *who* dimension constrains expressively focused campaign and marketing strategies.

culus is determined by the individual voter's preference for one candidate over another.

An individual i's utility for candidates X and Y holding office, given these candidates' policy stances, is determined by the difference between the voter's ideal point, Π_i^*, on the policy spectrum Π, and her utility for each candidate's policy positions. This is conveniently and most easily expressed in the negative absolute values of these differences: the greater the spatial distance between a candidate's position and the voter's ideal point, the smaller will be her utility for that candidate. The possible maximum for each of the policy-based utilities associated with each of the candidates is zero.

$$u_i^{\Pi x} = -|\Pi_i^x - \Pi_i^*| \tag{6.3}$$

$$u_i^{\Pi y} = -|\Pi_i^y - \Pi_i^*| \tag{6.4}$$

B_i^x represents the individual's preference for candidate X rather than Y holding office:

$$B_i^x = u_i^{\Pi x} - u_i^{\Pi y} \tag{6.5}$$

For spatial theorists, this represents the essence of a basic two-candidate model of vote choice. If candidate X's policy position is closer to the voter's ideal point than is candidate Y's, $B_i^x > 0$, and the voter will vote for X. If, on the other hand, candidate Y's policy position is closer to the voter's ideal point, $B_i^x < 0$, and the voter will vote for Y.

However, voters not only choose candidates, but make a compound decision involving both *whether to vote* and *whom to vote for*. Through substitution, the voter's preference over candidates can be included in the collective action expression of a voter's instrumental utility derived from voting for candidate X:

$$q_i^x = p(u_i^{\Pi x} - u_i^{\Pi y}) - C_i \tag{6.6}$$

From this equation we can identify some elementary conditions governing an individual voter's instrumentally driven vote decision.

To begin with, and most obviously, if the voter's policy preference is closer to the policy position of candidate Y than to the position of candidate X, then we are certain that $q_i^x < 0$, and the voter will not vote for candidate X. She may vote for candidate Y or altogether abstain from the election.

Conversely, if the voter's policy preference is closer to the position of candidate X than to that of Candidate Y, then q_i^x is either positive (if

$p(u_i^{\Pi x} - u_i^{\Pi y}) > C_i)$, or negative (if $p(u_i^{\Pi x} - u_i^{\Pi y}) < C_i)$. In the first case, instrumental returns will motivate the voter to vote for candidate X, and in the second case, instrumental returns will be insufficient and the voter will abstain from voting for candidate X, even though she prefers X to Y. In this latter case, the cost of voting outweighs the voter's expected benefit of voting for her preferred candidate.

This instrumental focus combines the spatial logic of voter choice with the collective action logic of voter turnout. We know from the collective action literature that the probability p of effecting an electoral outcome vanishes to zero as the electorate becomes large. Consequently, in large-scale elections, regardless of the individual voter's preference for the candidates' policy stance, her instrumental utility q_i^x approaches the value of $-C_i$, which means the voter receives only a disutility from voting for candidate X. In the private-good case of consumption of a material market good, in contrast, q_i^x can carry a positive value, as here $p = 1.0$: the consumer's participation is *certain* to provide her with the good. Here it is solely the relative magnitude of C_i (typically a compound of financial cost of the good and the additional effort of acquisition) which determines whether the consumer will choose to consume the good.

There are several reasons for keeping q_i^x in the utility function, even though the value of q_i^x in the large-scale electoral context is certain to approach the negative value of the cost of voting, thus ensuring that q_i^x will never singularly be responsible for a voter's participation. First, by keeping a more broadly specified expression, we can maintain the empirical comparative focus on electoral participation and market consumption introduced in chapter five: because $p = 1.0$ in the market context, q_i^x will play an important role in the decisions guiding the consumption of physcial private goods.

Second, retaining the instrumental component allows for the possibility that voters may exaggerate to themselves the degree of influence they have over the outcome of the election: as I discuss in the next chapter, voters simply may not be aware of the extreme irrelevance of their vote, and candidates deliberately may choose to exaggerate to voters the efficacy of their individual vote. In that event, q_i^x should reflect voters' perception of the instrumental, outcome-oriented benefit they derive from participation, which may in fact be greater than zero.

Third, retaining q_i^x in the model permits me to formalize the trade-off between producers' instrumental enhancement of goods or candidates, and the symbolic cost such strategic enhancement generates for those participants as a consequence. As I noted in chapter five and will explore in chapter seven (and as has long been known to marketing experts in the product realm), to make a good or candidate instrumentally more attractive inevitably will reduce that good's or candidate's symbolic value. An equivalent trade-off will be shown to exist in the electoral context.

Fourth, and most important, the very fact that q_i^x approaches $-C_i$ as the election becomes large posits a threshold: in addition to specifying that there is an expressive utility associated with voting, the presence of C_i gives us a sense of the magnitude this expressive utility must take on in order to drive the voter to the polling booth. As I will show toward the end of this chapter, it is this threshold function of the negative value of q_{ii}^x, in collective action, that most succinctly pitches instrumental and expressive utility against one another.

6.1.2 Assumptions

Contained in the simple model are three foundational assumptions, each of which will be relaxed later in this chapter.

First, on the instrumental side, I assume a *heterogeneity of participants' instrumental preferences*. Different participants will autonomously ascribe different pragmatic or instrumental preferences to products or activities, quite independently of (and in addition to) these products' or activities' expressive significances. This is consistent with the standard assumption of economists and spatial theorists, of the heterogeneity and exogeneity of preferences.

Second, on the expressive side, I begin by assuming that *all participants carry identical expressive preferences*. Currently all participants respond the same way to the number of electoral supporters for X. The expressive function f, consequently, does not carry the subscript i. As I will demonstrate, conclusions drawn from the assumption of identical preferences are remarkably robust when this assumption is relaxed. This is true, so long as the functional form we choose in our depictions in fact denotes a representative or "average" participant.

Third, I assume that *the expressive function is candidate or product specific*. Expressive intensity and the type of expressive appeal will vary among candidates. Different patterns of expressive returns consequently can be ascribed to the participation in different activities. To denote such product (or X-) specificity, the function f carries the subscript X.

I now define a representative individual's utility associated with voting for candidate X. I begin by aggregating individuals' utility functions, u_{ii}^x, to derive an aggregate utility function, U^x:[3]

---

[3] A potential complaint is that I am summing up different individuals' utilities to attain some aggregate measure of utility. Doing so, however, is no more contentious

$$U^x (n_x, q_i^x) = \sum_{i=1}^{n} \{f_x (n_x) + q_i^x\} \qquad (6.7)$$

$$= n \{f_x (n_x)\} + \sum_{i=1}^{n} q_i^x \qquad (6.8)$$

I subsequently derive a representative participant's utility function u_a^x by dividing the right-hand side by n:

$$u_a^x = f_x (n_x) + \frac{1}{n} \sum_{i=1}^{n} q_i^x \qquad (6.9)$$

$$= f_x (n_x) + q_a^x \qquad (6.10)$$

The term u_a^x denotes an "average" utility. Until I add the assumption that different participants carry different expressive utility functions, I will refer to this simple representative utility function.

6.1.3 Expressive Returns to Participation

First-Order Conditions. Expressive returns to participation can take on different shapes, as I noted in chapter four. The task now is to specify the ordinal conditions for expressive utility. To begin with, looking only at the first-order conditions of this utility function, there is a universe of only three possible relationships between the number of X-participants and the expressive value the individual associates with her own participation in X.

The relationship between an individual X-participant's utility and the number of X-participants may define a positive relationship as represented in the top panel of figure 6.1. This relationship typically is said to underlie the consumption of fashionable goods in the product market, which, accordingly, are referred to as "positive bandwagon" goods (Leibenstein 1950, 1976; Frank 1985; Bikhchandani, Hirshleifer, and Welch 1992). This shape has also been said to underlie the electoral support of presidential candidates across primaries (e.g., Bartels

---

than is microeconomists' notion of "consumer surplus," whereby individuals' utilities above their costs are summed to attain some aggregate surplus measure. Both there and for the instrumental component of this model, participants have varied preferences. The symbolic component of the model here, at present, still is identically defined for all participants and should therefore not pose a problem.

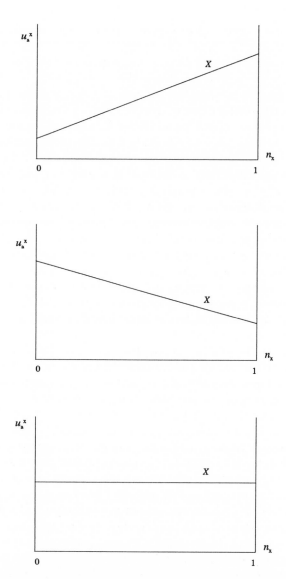

Figure 6.1: The three possible first-order conditions for a representative voter's expressive utility u_a^x associated with voting for a candidate X, as a function of the aggregate number of X-voters, n_x. In the first panel, an individual X-voter's utility increases with the number of X-voters. In the second panel, it decreases as the number of X-voters increases. And in the third panel, it remains invariant.

1988), and the support of candidates and elected officials in opinion polls published over time (e.g., Herbst 1993). The more individuals are seen to support the candidate, the greater the extent of an individual's support for that candidate will be.

The relationship between the number of X-participants and an individual X-participant's expressive utility may go the opposite way, as represented in the second panel of the figure. If the consumption of fashionable goods and the participation in fashionable activities might define the first scenario, the consumption of goods with more selective appeal has been said to define this scenario of the "snob" good (Leibenstein 1976). Here, witnessing high participation in fact reduces the utility an individual derives from her participation. Interestingly, political scientists who have detected the positive bandwagon component depicted in the first panel of figure 6.1 have also detected a negative bandwagon component for the same candidates. For example, as Bartels (1988, 44) notes, beyond some level of aggregate participation, the "story" begins to "wear thin". The implication is that above a certain level of aggregate participation, a representative voter derives less utility out of participation, as aggregate X-support levels continue to increase.

And, finally, the utility gained from participation may simply be invariant with aggregate participation levels, as in the bottom panel of figure 6.1. Here the value of participation is exogenous to participation levels: it does not matter how many voters vote for George Bush, or how many consumers are seen to participate in the consumption of Coca-Cola: the meaning of voting for the candidate or consuming the beverage does not change as the number of Bush supporters and Cola drinkers changes. This typology is interesting not because it is likely to exist in the expressive context—in the present use of the term, it would fail to be expressive if it did—but because it is likely to define the *idiom* in which an individual describes her preferences. Even if the reasons for an individual's participation in voting X are expressive and thus wound up in the aggregate level of (expected) X-participation, it is likely that the X-participant's stated reasons (that is, her reason*ing*), to others and to herself will take on an idiom that proclaims that her motivation was in fact unaffected by, and thus independent of, aggregate participation levels.

Second-Order Conditions. While I have identified the three possible first-order conditions for the relationship between the number of X-participants, n_x, and the representative individual's utility derived from her X-participation, u_a^x, none of these will adequately characterize an expressive benefit that is derived from attachment, either to a candidate or to his other supporters. To do so, we need to posit a second-order condition.

If expressive benefits are derived from "Being," or from attachment to a collective, then two closely related features matter to the voter. To vote for a candidate contains for the voter an understanding of what she *is*. Importantly, it will also contain for the same voter an understanding of what she *is not*. In the product market, wearing a fashionable item of clothing is desirable, both because it attaches you to some (however abstractly defined) similarly clad collective and, just as important, because it also contrasts you with a collective that is not dressed like you. Both of these relational aspects determine what your choice of clothing means.

For the expressive benefit of voting, similarly, looking only at information regarding the (alleged) number of current supporters of a candidate X, there will be an optimal proportion of the electorate $0 < n_x^* < 1$ at which voting for the candidate will generate the highest expressive utility, as in figure 6.2. For example, if the perceived support level were in fact at n_x^* (although there is nothing in our analysis that would suggest it need be), then the collective to which the voter attaches is defined by the interval $[0, n_x^*]$ whereas the collective with

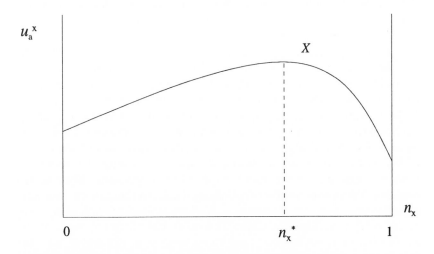

Figure 6.2: Second-order condition of expressive utility. Because the expressive utility associated with voting emerges from attachment to a collective of fellow voters, there will be some optimal attachment quantity of X-participants n_x^*, together with an optimal contrast-quantity $1 - n_x^*$, for which the individual's utility associated with X-voting will be the highest.

which the voter contrasts herself is defined by $[n_x^*,1]$. The relationship between the expressive voter's utility and the number of fellow voters for the same candidate is therefore *necessarily nonmonotonic*. This condition is further emphasized by an investigation of the extreme points: at $n_x = 0$, expressive attachment is unlikely to generate expressive benefit, as there is nobody to associate with, and at $n_x = 1$ there is nobody to distinguish yourself from, which in itself makes the notion of attachment nonsensical.[4]

Finally, we can make no strong predictions about the precise location of the peak of the X-voter's utility, n_x^*, as determined by the aggregate number of participants n_x. The otherwise diverse writings of Bartels, Edelman, Herbst, and Popkin all suggest that, typically, the utility of voting for a candidate is particularly high when he is likely to win, but when he is not saturated with electoral support. This implies that the peak of the utility curve lies to the right of the 0.5 mark, if there are two candidates. In addition, we can infer that candidates will attempt to present themselves in a manner that corresponds to a high n_x value corresponding to that peak: we might argue that for the candidate to emphasize that he is already winning is for him to define not just the present location of the electorate along the curve, but also to try to define the shape of the curve itself. It is for him to define himself as a majority candidate, and for him to signal to the collective of prospective voters that to belong to this larger collective is attractive.

6.1.4 Restrictions through Nonambiguity

In addition, and more systematically, the location of the peak will also be a function of the *who* dimension described in chapter four. I noted in the jukebox model of chapter two and in the comparative history of chapter five that in large-scale settings, producers of participation typically stress the high level of aggregate participation (*how many*), while at the same time shielding prospective participants from the exact identity characteristics of those other participants (they shield the *who*). Beyond a certain level of aggregate participation, the exact identity of participants becomes a liability, as the variation in identity of the collective becomes large. The more specific an identity reference of fellow X-participants, the more specific or nonambiguous the

---

[4] The contrasting interval $[n_x^*,1]$, differentiates this type of externality from network externalities identified by industrial organization theorists, where benefits are derived only from coordination: to return to the examples used in chapter three, the more people use the QWERTY keyboard or the VHS video system, the greater the benefit to individual QWERTY and VHS users respectively (David 1985; Tirole 1988, 404).

association of *what it means to be* an X-participant. Consequently, the more selective expressive identification necessarily will be.

The same logic applies not only to the role of ambiguity along the *who* dimension, but to ambiguity of the candidate himself, which I discussed in chapter four as "polysemy." The more strategically ambiguous a candidate, the greater the variety of reasons through which individuals can attach to him with their participation. Therefore, though I have yet more carefully to explore the relationship between the *who* and an individual's expressive utility, I should note for now that the location of the peak n_x^* will in part be determined by the *who* dimension and the degree of its shielding, as well as by the degree of polysemy. The less narrowly defined the identity specification for a prospective participant (that is, when the extent of shielding and the degree of polysemy are high), the further to the right will the peak reside.

Consequently, to follow the intuition of the political scientists previously cited, and matching Bartels's description of a saturation point somewhere above the majority quantity of a candidate's electoral support, I will specify ordinal conditions matching those of the curve of figure 6.2. As I do so, I will also investigate the sensitivity of my predictions to the precise location of n_x^*. As we shall see, these predictions are quite robust to variations in these specifications.

6.1.5   Expressive Tipping

In order to predict how aggregate voting is likely to develop on the basis of the identified expressive utility curves, and to avoid the error of simply translating individuals' preference maps onto collectively derived outcomes, I superimpose a choice component. Assume we have two candidates, X and Y, for whom all individuals carry identical preference curves, as displayed in figure 6.2. Further assume for now that all voters are purely expressive and are purely expressive in exactly the same way. Finally, assume for now that everybody votes: the choice is truly binary, as abstention is not an option. (I relax all three assumptions below.)

Because the range of aggregate participation in X can be read from left to right, the number of Y-participants can be read off the same axis from right to left (Schelling 1978, 243). As I standardize the axis to range from 0 to 1, any quantity n_x will represent the number of X-participants, whereas the remaining quantity of participants $1 - n_x$ will represent the number of Y-participants: in this simple binary choice setting, participating in X is equivalent to not participating in Y, and vice versa. By that very logic the Y-preference curve, which defines the same shape as the X-preference curve, can be represented on the same graph as a flipped image of the X-curve.

Three distinct equilibria can be found in figure 6.3. For any $n_x < n_x^k$, participating in Y is preferable, for the individual voter, to participating in X. Consequently, for a starting value for the number of X-voters smaller than n_x^k, individuals will choose to participate in voting Y, not X, until they reach the equilibrium quantity n_x^t, the point at which candidate Y takes a stable lead and X trails. For any starting value for the number of X-voters greater than n_x^k, aggregate participation levels will equilibrate at n_x^l, where candidate X takes a stable lead. Both n_x^t and n_x^l are stable equilibria, in that any small displacements away from these outcomes will result in a return to them. The dividing equilibrium n_x^k is unstable, for a displacement in the direction of greater X-participation results in a stable n_x^l-outcome, whereas a displacement in the opposite direction will result in a stable n_x^t-outcome. The unstable equilibrium point n_x^k, in Schelling's (1978) terms, is a "tipping point."

6.1.6 Ordinal Robustness

Three ordinal conditions determine the location of equilibria in this model. An investigation of these conditions will determine the extent to which these initial results are generalizable.

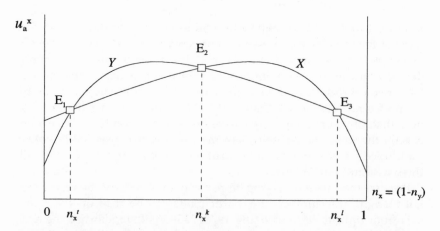

Figure 6.3: For any initial quantity of aggregate X-voting $n_x > n_x^k$ aggregate voting levels will equilibrate at n_x^l, with X taking a lead. For any initial quantity of aggregate X-voting $n_x < n_x^k$, aggregate voting levels will equilibrate at n_x^t, with X trailing. The participation level n_x^k defines an unstable equilibrium, or "tipping" point.

The first condition that matters concerns the location of the two curves' peaks. Provided that the two curves intersect, the only requirement for there to be a single tipping point E_2 that divides the two stable equilibria E_1 and E_3, is the YX sequence of these peaks along the n_x dimension.[5] The intersection need not be in the center, which means that the curves need not be symmetrical. If the sequence of the peaks is reversed, we find one stable equilibrium point at their central intersection, and the two surrounding intersection points are both unstable equilibria.

This takes us to the second condition that determines outcomes— the location of the tipping crossover point. For example, if that point resides in the low-n_x region, then candidate X will enjoy the benefit of momentum starting with relatively low aggregate support levels.

Finally, the locations of the stable equilibrium points E_1 and E_3 are determined by the presence of intersection points in addition to the tipping point. If the saturation effect is very strong, then these additional points of intersection will exist, as the individual's X-participation utility curve drops more quickly beyond the saturation point. But note that E_1 and E_3 exist regardless of this extreme saturation effect: in the absence of these saturation-specific additional points of intersection, E_1 will reside where $n_x = 0$, and E_3 will reside where $n_x = 1$. *Consequently, all conclusions I draw from a depiction involving saturation-specific stable equilibria will still hold when no such crossover points exist*: in these cases, E_1 and E_3 will simply go to the bounding values of 0 and 1 respectively.

These strictly ordinal specifications are easily represented in the generalizable depiction of figure 6.4. (Because we need only the ordinal conditions, I simplify figure 6.3 by using straight lines to denote the relationship between the three conditional points that define each of the utility curves.)

The lower panel of the figure expresses X-participation levels along its horizontal axis and Y-participation levels along its vertical axis. Currently, since we are still dealing with a full-participation binary setting, where participation in Y is equivalent to not participating in X, we know that all outcomes, regardless of whether they are equilibria, necessarily lie on the diagonal connecting the two (n_x, n_y) points $(0,1)$ and $(1,0)$.

The three equilibria identified in this figure are functionally equivalent to those depicted in figure 6.3, as are the "gravitational" ranges

---

[5] I switch from the notation n_x^t and n_x^l to E_1 and E_3, as these two stable equilibria need not necessarily denote candidate-X-leading and candidate-X-trailing quantities in the same way.

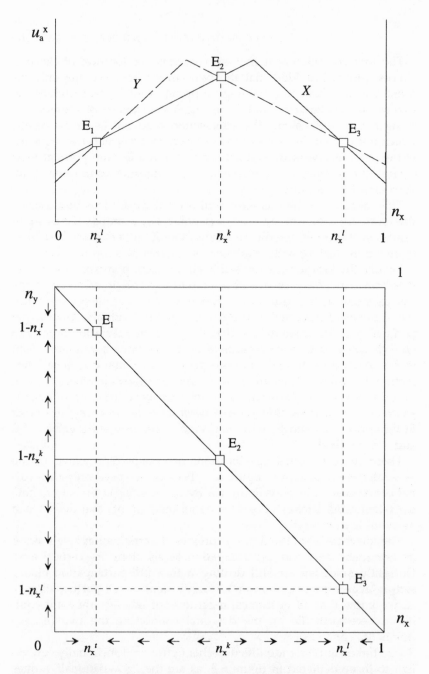

Figure 6.4: Ordinal conditions of expressive tipping. Provided each candidate's individual-level, average-voter utility shape intersects the opponent's curve from below while that candidate's own number of supporters is increasing, an unstable equilibrium point E_2 (at n_x^k) exists. In the presence of a strong saturation effect, two additional stable equilibrium points exist, shown by E_1 and E_3. In the absence of a strong saturation effect, these two stable-equilibrium points take on the values of $n_x = 0$ (for E_1) and $n_x = 1$ (for E_3).

depicted along the Y- and X-participation axes. Additionally, this graph is conveniently capable of representing a host of different utility shapes for X, with the minimum proviso that, at some point, they intersect the utility curve for Y from underneath. If, in addition, the saturation effect of the representative X-voter's utility is strong enough for the X-curve to intersect the Y-curve once again, from above, the stable equilibrium quantity n_x^l (corresponding to the stable equilibrium point E_3) will be greater than n_x^k and n^*, but smaller than 1: the outcome would be equivalent to that depicted in figure 6.3. As I have noted, in the absence of so strong a saturation effect, E_3 still exists, although it will be at the point where *all* individuals participate in X and none participate in Y, at the point $(1,0)$.

This analysis tells us that the sequence of the X- and Y-peaks determines the general characteristics of the tipping dynamic. In fact, it can very easily be shown that for expressive curves with a YX sequence of peaks over n_x, the dynamic is a specific version of a pure positive-bandwagon tipping model based on two intersecting utility curves of the top panel of figure 6.1. This produces one unstable equilibrium tipping point, surrounded to the left and right by two stable equilibria. Conversely, an XY sequence of peaks produces a dynamic that is related to the intersection of two "snob-good" curves in the second panel of figure 6.1. Here we derive one stable equilibrium point. Consequently, our use of the particular utility shape introduced in figure 6.2, provided we have good reason to assume a YX sequence of peaks, is robust to a wide range of utility specifications sharing only a very minimal set of ordinal assumptions.

6.2   Varied Preferences and Turnout

Until now I have assumed that voters' preferences are purely expressive, and are identically so, and that all prospective voters participate in the election. Both assumptions are unrealistic and will now be relaxed.

6.2.1   Varied Preferences

Three reasons make the assumption of preference homogeneity unrealistic. First, among voters who are expressive, it would be unrealistic to assume that all of them are expressive in the same way. Even in the present single-parameter world, where the visible level of a candidate's electoral support determines the expressive utility of voting, different expressive voters will be characterized by a variety of locations of the X-voting preference curve's peak n_x^* (in figure 6.2), as well as of the tipping point n_x^k (in figure 6.3). The very definition of expressive utility, as discussed in chapter four, is that different expressive voters will hold different private meanings for voting for the same candidate. Consequently, we must allow for the fact that the same type of information regarding a candidate's current level of aggregate electoral support will have different expressive consequences for different voters. Formally, the expressive function f should now carry an additional subscript i:

$$u_i^x (n, q_i^x) = f_{xi} (n_x) + q_i^x \qquad (6.11)$$

Second, we should not assume that all voters are expressive. As I noted in the very beginning of this book, the purpose here is to identify the weaknesses of instrumentally based theories of voting and take up the cues of political scientists since (and including) Downs who have argued that there will likely be an expressive motivation to voting, too. It is not to replace one universal motivation by positing another and thus to insist that all voters are purely expressive. Analytically, this suggests that we need to explore the robustness of an expressively based method to the assumption of variability of voter motivation.

Third, and finally, in the initial tipping model I have assumed universal turnout. For all the reasons noted in chapter three, this assumption is simply unrealistic, regardless of the type of motivation we infer on behalf of voters. Some voters will find both candidates sufficiently unappealing not to want to attach to either of them, or to their respective supporting collectives. Among voters who reason their participation in strictly instrumental terms, there will be those who regard the instrumental insufficiency of the vote in determining the electoral outcome as reason not to vote.

Fortunately, all three assumptions relating to preference homogeneity on the one hand and universal turnout on the other can simultaneously be relaxed if we simply assume that the tipping point is variable, rather than fixed. This makes for remarkable simplicity and efficiency.

First, to note that expressive voters respond differently to information regarding candidates' aggregate support is to note that the location of n_x^k varies for these voters across the entire [0,1] interval.

Second, to note that some voters are not expressive means that they do not respond to variations in n_x: they will either *vote* for X, regardless of candidate X's current support levels, or they will *not vote* for X (that is, vote for Y or not vote at all), regardless of support levels. This exogeneity is formally equivalent to saying that for some voters the location of the tipping point n_x^k is at $n_x = 0$, and for some voters the tipping point n_x^k lies at $n_x = 1$.[6]

Third, and similarly, for those whose participation is determined by other factors, we can again assume a distribution of n_x^k: instrumentally superrational collective action theorists will vote only when n_x^k is *exactly* equal to 0.5 (because it practically never is, they practically never do). It may be, alternatively, that some voters who have a gambling preference enjoy voting only when the current support level for each candidate is within a few points of that same quantity: playing in an election is simply more exciting when the game is less predictable.

It is easy to slip into speculation about what may affect individuals' motivation along the n_x dimension. All the more important that analytically we can simultaneously relax a diverse set of conditions by assuming that the tipping point n_x^k takes on different values for different voters. The very fact that we do not need to distinguish between substantively diverse types of reasons as we assume a distribution for this single parameter strengthens our analytical leverage.

For simple illustration, compare two voters: Type I, who carries perfectly symmetric preferences for candidates X and Y; and Type II, who has a higher disposition toward candidate Y. Both are represented in figure 6.5 (ignore, for now, the horizontal dotted line, as well as the curves for Y_1 and Y_2). If we are in a full-participation world, Type II will vote for Y, regardless, which is identical to saying that for Type II, $n_x^k = 1$. Type I will vote for X or Y, depending on current candidate-support levels. Note that we can no longer instantly identify electoral equilibria on this graph: we are no longer assuming that all voters have identical tipping motivations, but are instead contrasting two particular types of voters. Although we can make predictions how they would vote, given aggregate information regarding electoral preferences, we cannot identify equilibria unless we know the distribution of tipping points for the population.

6.2.2 Turnout: Instrumental and Expressive Returns

The functional form f_{xi} defines the ordinal conditions of the X-voter's expressive utility. In the previous section, as we began to allow for different autonomous heights for different X-voters' utility, we essentially allowed for the fact that different voters will experience and

---

[6] Strictly, of course, there no longer is a tipping point for these voters, as they are nonresponsive (or "parametric") to variations in n_x. We can, however, include these voters in the tipping model, by ascribing to them pseudo-tipping quantities at the two extreme points.

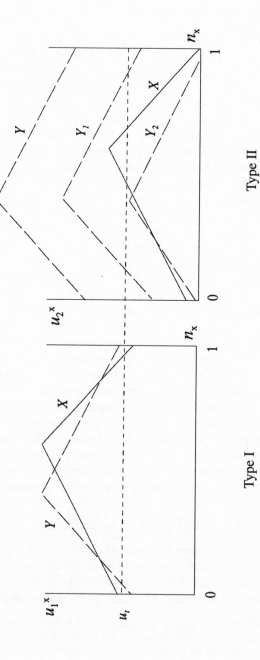

Type I   Type II

Figure 6.5: Two voter types. Type I carries symmetric preference for candidates X and Y, and Type II is disposed toward Y, in the Y- and Y_1-curves, and toward X, in the Y_2-curve of the right-hand panel. Positing an instrumental, exogenous disutility threshold for voting allows us to approach voter choice and voter turnout simultaneously.

express different extents of attachment to their preferred candidates. Substantively, this means that some voters will find it more attractive to be identified as an X-supporter than will others. A straightforward conclusion is that those whose desire for attachment is lower will be less likely to turn out and vote for their preferred candidate: if you don't much like the candidate, you will carry no desire in shaping your own political identity through an expressive attachment to him.

As we turn our attention to voter turnout, as the collective action literature teaches us and as our initial model specification reflects, we need to combine both our instrumental and expressive focus. In equation 6.6 I posited an instrumental return function for voter participation and noted how, as elections grow in size, q_i^x approaches $-C_i$. Analytically, this condition is captured if we posit a utility threshold: if the individual voter's utility derived from an expressive attachment to the candidate fails to outweigh the negative value of q_i^x, she will not vote for him. Assume that for both Type I and Type II in figure 6.5, q_i^x defines the threshold u_t, and that Type II's Y-participant utility is defined by the Y-curve. Here, both voters will still vote for their preferred candidates: Type II will vote for Y, and Type I will vote either for X or Y, depending on where perceived X- and Y-support levels are, respectively.

Now assume that Type II's Y-participants' utility instead is defined by the Y_1-curve. Provided that the share of aggregate Y-support lies in the range in which that voter's Y-utility curve is above u_t, Type II will vote for Y. Prior and beyond that, she will abstain from voting altogether (because her X-utility is lower still). If Type II carries a Y-utility curve as defined by Y_2, she will not vote for Y, regardless, though she may vote for X, depending on current X-/Y-support levels.

A realistic interpretation of this depiction would be that in this single-parameter world, prospective voters respond to polling information concerning the relative standing of two candidates among the electorate: they respond to the share (or percentage) of approval for that candidate among the population. The *motivational trigger* is still binary, as they respond to information concerning how the population's relative support for the two candidates divides. These individuals' electoral *action*, on the other hand, can now take on three values. As before, they may vote for either X or Y. In addition, however, they now may also choose to abstain. Given that the trigger remains binary, we can continue to use the tipping depiction.

6.2.3   A Heterogeneous Tipping Model

I have defined a world in which citizens respond to information regarding candidates' support levels in the population, and where the utility of voting over some disutility threshold determines whether citizens vote for their preferred candidate. I have noted that citizens will hold different expressive incentives and that we should also allow for them to hold some nonexpressive incentives.

As I have noted, the assumption that different voters provide their electoral support on the basis of different types of motivation can be formalized by a distribution of the tipping point n_x^k across the entire n_x range [0,1]. I have captured this to a small extent by proposing two voters with different tipping points. I now offer a fuller presentation by allowing for a continuum of different crossover points across the population.

For the sake of simplicity, assume a distribution of n_x^k for different voters i, which roughly approximates a truncated normal distribution, with its mean at 0.5, and its truncation at 0 and 1. Substantively, this means that most voters have their tipping point somewhere around the 50 percent mark, even though n_{xi}^k is distributed across the entire [0,1] range. Because we do not care about the actual density of voters for each potential value of n_x^k, which is the number of voters for whom a particular value represents the switch-over point from Y to X, but care instead about the number of voters for whom a particular value of n_x^k is *sufficient* to vote for X rather than Y, we require a cumulative density function.

The horizontal axis of figure 6.6 measures the *perceived* level of candidate X's electoral support, and the vertical axis measures his *actual* support: the logic is "iterative" in that voters receive, from the media or from the campaign, poll information in the period leading up to the election (a horizontal adjustment), then subsequently react to this information by adjusting their own support (vertical adjustment), which in turn leads to a (horizontal) adjustment in poll information, to which voters again respond in the next round (vertically). The vertical distance $\overline{OA}$ depicts the number of citizens who prefer X, no matter what, whereas the vertical distance $\overline{BZ}$ depicts the number of citizens who support Y, no matter what. K is a cumulative tipping point: for any quantity n_x greater than K, support will equilibrate at the higher X-support level X^*, whereas for any quantity shy of K, support will equilibrate at the lower X- (that is, higher Y-) support level Y^*.

This model again shows that our original predictions regarding support levels in a homogeneous, all-expressive preference setting are

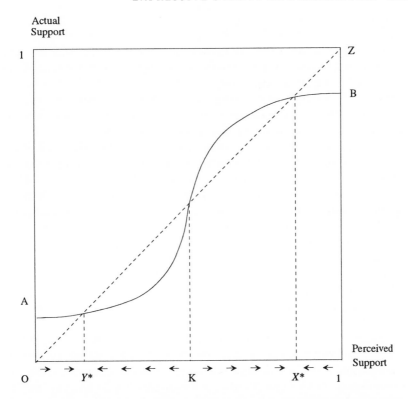

Figure 6.6: Heterogeneous expressive tipping model. The S-shaped curve represents a cumulative density function, derived from a distribution of individual-level utility cross-over points and denoting the number of voters for whom a particular X-support level is sufficient to induce their participation. Y^* and X^* are heterogeneous equivalences of the stable equilibrium quantities E_1 and E_3 in the identical-preference depictions of the previous figures. K, similarly, is a heterogeneous-preference equivalent of the identical-preference tipping point n_x^k of the previous figures.

quite robust and allow themselves to be translated in a heterogeneous-preference model. The extent to which voters are insensitive
to aggregate support levels will be depicted by the autonomous vertical distances at both ends of the cumulative density function. Better
still, we can draw our predictions without needing to identify formally the extent to which these vertical distances are composed of
voters who support their preferred candidates for staunch expressive
reason, or for nonexpressive reasons. What drives momentum in this
model is the component of the electorate that responds to poll information, as our theory of expressive motivation would lead us to expect, and the smaller the proportion of the population that is expres-

sive, the more narrow the range that separates X^* and Y^*. This depiction demonstrates how the conclusions drawn from a model in which all voters are expressively motivated are quite robust and are still relevant in a model in which only a proportion of the electorate is guided by expressive motivation.

Finally, by turning to the heterogeneous tipping model, we cannot associate with the equilibrium quantities any specific levels of turnout. To do so requires us to disaggregate the heterogeneous model into individual voter-type depictions, as I did earlier. This earlier exercise does, however, allow us to draw inferences about turnout levels if we know how the equilibria were generated in the first place. As I will discuss in chapters seven and eight, for example, if these equilibria result from a campaign strategy designed to alter the height of the voter's curve for *either* candidate (for example, through negative campaigning), then this will alter overall turnout in the identical direction.

6.3 DISCUSSION: MOMENTUM

The model I have presented in this chapter suggests that if we define expressive motivation as guided by "Being"—that is, the participation of voters and consumers is motivated by a form of expressive attachment—we can specify for a representative or "average" participant a utility curve that carries a peak somewhere between support levels of $n_x = 0$ and $n_x = 1$. If we make some additional assumptions concerning candidates' successful restrictive use of the *who* dimension, then we can additionally locate the peak of the utility curve (in a two-candidate setting) to the right of the majority point. This very minimal analytical specification is sufficient to generate the prediction that there will be electoral momentum. As I also showed, that prediction is robust to the assumption of heterogeneous preferences. All that is required is that for at least one of the candidates, the average participant's expressive peak lies beyond the 0.5 mark in a two-candidate election. Therefore, the model I presented shows that even the most minimal expressive assumption among individual prospective participants will lead us to predict the existence of bandwagons at the collective level.

We know from the empirical literature that these electoral bandwagons do, in fact, exist. For the remainder of this chapter, I will discuss, first, some of the empirical evidence on electoral momentum at the collective level; second, the insufficiency of existing instrumentally and non-instrumentally-based explanations that have been provided for electoral momentum; and, third, the difficulties associated with empirical measurement of *who* it is, precisely, that is most expressive—that is, most responsive to information concerning aggregate support. I focus primarily on the empirical work of Bartels (1988), but also on more recent approaches by Cox (1997), Alvarez and Nagler (2000), and Morton (1991). In my discussion of difficulties associated with measurement I refer to King (1997) and to Penubarti and Schuessler (1999).

6.3.1   Aggregate Momentum

One of the most eloquent and methodologically sophisticated empirical studies of aggregate-level electoral momentum is to be found in the work of Bartels (1988), who identified the presence of "momentum" in the support of candidates across presidential primaries. Showing how the popularity of a candidate may "pick up" early on in an electoral contest, this increase in support may itself generate further support among the electorate, eventually resulting in the candidate's electoral victory. Due to the media's, and by extension the public's, focus on the "horse race" nature of the electoral contest, opinion polls serve not only as a measure of increase in broad support, but also as a *stimulus* for further support of a candidate among the public. Electoral victories, such as Jimmy Carter's in the 1976 presidential election, are to a large extent attributed to successes in early primaries. On the basis of such identified momentum, the modeling of strategic campaign spending and the like by other political scientists has frequently prescribed heavier spending by the campaign manager during early primaries, as the resultant successes would in themselves generate further victories in subsequent primaries and, eventually, in the general election (Brams and Davis 1982).

According to Bartels, there are four separate sources to the momentum or bandwagon preferences of individual voters, two of which are instrumentally based, and two of which are not.

First, on the instrumental side, prospective voters rationally avoid "wasting" their votes. Any predisposition an individual voter may have toward a particular candidate will more likely translate into participation if that candidate stands a chance of winning to begin with. The concern for vote wasting may be sufficiently strong for the individual participant to be more inclined to vote for his or her second choice in the presidential primary, if that less-preferred candidate stands a greater chance of winning against the opposing party's candidate in the general election. Electoral participation in the primaries, therefore, allegedly may represent a form of *strategic* or *sophisticated* voting.

A second instrumental reason for voters to jump on the bandwagon is that visible support levels may serve as simple cues for individuals to conclude that their own as yet uncertain political leanings toward a candidate may be "right." High aggregate support, therefore, serves as an uncostly proxy source of information to the individual voter about a candidate's likely quality. As I noted in chapter three, the resultant bandwagon effects are comparable to those identified by scholars as "informational cascades," where a voter's or consumer's (potentially arbitrary) choice of one candidate or product over another generates an informational externality and will increase the likelihood of others participation also.

Third and fourth, a nonrational set of explanations is proposed by Bartels in the form of "contagion" effects on the one hand and the desire to "support a winner" on the other. Contagion refers to a form of herding behavior among prospective voters due to some other-than outcome-oriented motivation, and the alleged desire to support a winner, too, refers to the presence of some voter preference that, in itself, is irreducible.

All four reasons share the notion that preferences are endogenous to the context of participation itself: all describe how individuals' witnessing of a collective's participation will determine aggregate participation levels in the instant future. In contrast to these endogenous factors, Bartels also mentions a second motivational source, namely that of individuals' "political disposition." This is the functional equivalent of the instrumental component here in that it refers to a set of tastes or preferences that exists both prior to and independent of the level of aggregate participation. Consistent with the division I proposed in the model of this chapter, such preferences are *exogenous*. In contrast to the endogenous bandwagon effects, which Bartels considers "shared," these exogenous preferences vary among participants.

Although this work shares with Bartels the distinction between the endogenous and exogenous motivations underlying participation, it differs in its methodological orientation at the microlevel. For reasons I noted in chapter three, these microlevel reasons are insufficient in explaining the electoral bandwagons that are observable at the aggregate level.

First and foremost, Bartels's rationally based instrumental factors should be constrained by the participation paradox much as other instrumental approaches are. This applies both to his explanation concerning participants' strategic avoidance of vote wasting, as well as to their search for (uncostly) information. To begin with, if strategic intent denotes sophisticated, nonmyopic, forward-looking behavior, then voters in presidential elections will have two potential free-rider environments to contend with: one rooted in the context of the primaries, the other rooted in the general election. Regardless of whether participants' rational concern is with vote wasting or with cheap information gathering, they will face a rational disincentive in knowing that their individual vote will be instrumentally irrelevant. Furthermore, if outcome-oriented concerns were indeed the only relevant motivation to prospective participants, momentum effects should appear only if candidates approach the margin required to secure electoral victory. As I demonstrated in chapter three, any other range will almost certainly render the individual vote either insufficient if it supports the trailing candidate, or redundant if it supports the frontrunner. As Bartels himself argues, however, momentum may appear in any range along the spectrum of a candidate's public support.

On the noninstrumental side, Bartels mentions contagion and the desire to vote for a winner as codetermining the bandwagon component of individual voters' preferences. Both of these are perhaps consistent with the theoretical orientation of the present work and may be inherently correct. Despite this descriptive appropriateness, however, neither offers much of an *explanation* beyond presenting itself as an irreducible preference.

The criticism levied against Bartels's instrumental explanation can also be applied to the more recent work of Cox (1997), Morton (1991), and Alvarez and Nagler (2000). A now very active interest of political economists studying electoral behavior is with the strategic coordination of voters. Much in line with Bartels's explanation that voters avoid "wasting" their votes on candidates who have no chance of winning the election, for Cox and others, voters coordinate their vote choice so as to maximize the potency of their vote: quite frequently, they will vote for their second-preferred candidate in order both to avoid the victory of a lesser-preferred candidate and to avoid wasting their vote on their most-preferred candidate, who stands no chance of winning the election.

Using data gathered from electoral systems across the globe, Cox treats as evidence for such strategic voting the convergence of vote intentions in the period leading up to an election. Morton bases her analysis of voters in American elections the same way. Alvarez and Nagler, in their analysis of Californian exit poll data seek evidence for sophisticated strategic voter choice by means of a cleverly designed survey instrument that attempts to reconstruct such strategic behavior by asking voters questions that may reflect the motivation behind their vote choice. (In their study, the fact that a high proportion of respondents were not able to answer the surveyor's questions because they were too difficult may suggest that the expectation of sophisticated strategic reasoning may simply be too high.)

In all these cases, to refer back to the discussion of chapter three, there seems to be an inconsistency in any argument claiming that voters' vote *choice* is guided by a desire to maximize the electoral impact of the vote while failing simultaneously to recognize the resultant explicit redundancy of the vote: the very information of other voters' voting intentions that is said to guide individual voters' coordination should at the same time tell these voters that their individual votes are irrelevant. There clearly is coordination among these voters, as both Bartels and Cox convincingly and eloquently demonstrate. It cannot, however, be simple concern with vote efficacy that motivates such coordination among voters.

6.3.2 Microlevel Momentum Preference

It should be stressed that tipping models as used in the present analysis themselves represent a form of coordination game. The primary difference here is the theoretical basis that is said to underlie individual voters' utility curves in the tipping depictions.[7] The theory of expressive motivation presented here provides an alternative microfoundation to the aggregate-level observation of electoral and consumer market momentum. In one important respect this approach is consistent with that of rational, social, and public choice theorists in that it *aggregates individual preferences to generate aggregate-level predictions.* At the same time, in this expressive context, aggregate-level support determines individual-level support for candidates. In a much broader sense than we normally employ, the concern here is with social equilibria generated by this endogeneity. This very same preference endogeneity is also what makes it difficult to seek empirical evidence for the existence of individual-level expressive preferences.

In the expressive context, this question amounts to asking about individual opinion holders' responsiveness to others' opinions: how sensitive is the expressive voter to aggregate preference levels, as expressed in opinion polls? Beyond recognizing momentum in a variety

[7] There is an additional, much more subtle difference. Tipping models share with coordination games the notion that players' payoffs are correlated: part of the utility is derived from making the same choice as others. On the other hand, coordination games tend to represent *strategic* interactions, whereas the behavior depicted in tipping games tends to be *reactive* to others' behavior.

of electoral settings, this is traditionally considered an unanswerable question. Specifically, to estimate statistically the effects of aggregate opinion on individuals' opinion formation is in practice to attempt to estimate the effects of polls on polls, which, of course, is impossible. Polls are the trigger (that is, independent) variable that explains the dependent variable, which, too, is measured in the form of polls. The problem once again is one of endogeneity or simultaneity.

Two possible methodological avenues exist for future empirical estimation of bandwagon responsiveness. First, with recent advances in ecological inference estimation, scholars have access to increasingly sophisticated methods of uncovering individual-level behavior from aggregate-level data (Schuessler 1999). Specifically, a relevant extension of King's (1997) ecological inference solution EI is found in ecological panel inference, or EPI (Penubarti and Schuessler 1999). EPI allows scholars to investigate which parts of the population are most reactive to aggregate-level movement of public opinion in forming their own opinion. With further development, this indicates a promising future in identifying empirically how tipping points are distributed across a population to form the hetergeneous tipping model discussed in section 6.2. A second empirical possibility is found in experimentation: experiments allow us to expose subjects to aggregate-level information and to measure their responses directly. In other words, they allow us to break out of the endogeneity, as we are allowed to separate the trigger and the response. This, too, is the subject of future experimental research.

6.4   Conclusion

The investigation of this chapter has shown how a minimal operationalizing of an expressive dimension gives rise to a prediction of electoral bandwagons. The analysis shows that the presence and characteristics of these bandwagons is determined by the shape of individual participants' utility curves. With minimal assumptions about the expressive determinants of participants' utility (where these assumptions are derived from stylized social theory), the prediction of electoral momentum is generated. In a manner consistent with the approach of social choice theorists, this prediction of macrolevel momentum is derived from microlevel assumptions. Throughout the analysis I have paid particular attention to model robustness, showing that predictions of (1) identical and (2) all-expressive preferences across an entire voter population will also apply for a population wherein only a fraction of voters are expressive, and wherein they are differently so. This allows me, in the analysis of the next two chapters for the most part to remain with the simplified-assumption (and -depiction) approach.

The analysis of this chapter now enables us to specify producer interests and thus formally to approach expressively driven campaigning and marketing. I have identified the parameters that give rise to expressively focused bandwagons, and in the next two chapters I can identify which of these parameters are within the strategic reach of producers of participation. Consequently, I will be able to establish what an expressively focused campaign or marketing strategy will look like. I begin, in the next chapter, by noting how instrumentally focused strategies will change the composition of participants' utility. As I will show, instrumental enhancement of participation comes at an expressive cost: the electoral support of candidates with lower expressive content will be more volatile than of those whose expressive content is very high. This condition, long familiar to scholars and practitioners of marketing in the realm of mass consumption can be established in the electoral context, even with the simple tools assembled here. In chapter eight I continue my analysis of electoral campaigning and industrial marketing as I investigate the nature of expressively focused strategies of eliciting participation. Here the producer's strategic focus rests on a manipulation of participants' expressive function f_x. I will show (and reproduce from the historical account of chapter five) why an expressively focused strategy always will be more effective in raising aggregate participation levels when the size of the collective is large—regardless of whether that collective is a market or an electorate.

Chapter Seven

INSTRUMENTAL ENHANCEMENT

AND ITS EXPRESSIVE COSTS

> No one goes there anymore—it's too crowded.
> *(Yogi Berra, referring to a restaurant)*

> Camel Filters. They're not for everybody. (But then,
> they don't try to be.)
> *(Advertisement)*

I N THIS chapter and the next I turn my attention to the production of mass participation, in the form of electoral mass campaigning and industrial mass marketing. I first look at instrumentally focused campaign strategy (this chapter) and then at expressively focused campaigning (chapter eight). If the simple formalization of the previous chapter defines the "demand" dimension to expressively motivated participation, I now turn to investigate its "supply" dimension. I do so predominantly by introducing costs associated with the production of mass participation.

Specifically, in this chapter I investigate the producer's instrumentally focused campaign strategies *in an expressive context.* For reasons I noted in chapter two, an investigation of the instrumental domain should not occur in isolation from an analytical awareness of the realm of expressive motivation, and vice versa. As I will show here, instrumentally focused producer strategy inevitably results in a reduction of participants' expressive utility. This trade-off is known to scholars of marketing who have shown in the mass-market context how what they call the "commodification" (debranding or deidentification) of goods comes at the cost of high price sensitivity and low product loyalty (see my account in chapter five of Pepsi-Cola's initial attempt to compete with Coca-Cola on the basis of price in the early 1930s). As I will show in this chapter, an equivalent conclusion can be found for candidate support in the context of instrumentally focused campaigning. This conclusion is available only if such campaigning is studied in an expressive context.

In part 1 of this book and in the historical account of chapter five I have argued that producers of electoral mass participation are required to use expressively focused campaign strategy in order (1) to overcome the collective action problem by providing returns to participation—that is, to overcome individual voters' instrumentally defined cost of participation; and (2) to overcome the preference diversity of the electorate. In this chapter I take this conclusion one step further: not only are candidates better served through an expressive focus for these reasons, but they are required to *avoid a strictly instumental focus* in their campaign strategy. As I demonstrate here using the analytical tools established in the previous chapter, both in product marketing and in electoral campaigning, to make candidates or goods instrumentally more attractive will destroy their expressive value. Specifically, a strategy of instrumental enhancement washes out expressive utility. I will call this effect "expressive crowding out," and it is nicely captured by Yogi Berra's statement in the opening quote of this chapter. I close the chapter with a brief discussion of how "commodification" as understood by marketing practitioners and scholars is the exact opposite of "commodification" as understood by social theorists, whose definition is much closer to the approach pursued here. Beginning with Karl Marx's focus on the commodity and on commodity fetishism, and through the French social thought of Marcel Mauss (1967) and Emile Durkheim (1960) on the "social life of things" (Appadurai 1986) and on consumption as a socially defining act (Bourdieu 1984; Haug 1986; Lipovetsky 1994), physical goods become expressive (and thus are commodities) precisely because they *provide identity* for their consumers. I return to this discussion in the concluding chapter.

The trade-off between instrumental enhancement and expressive cost can be illustrated with analytical tools available from simple microeconomics. Using the same tools, I will also show how the practice of negative campaigning—making one's opponent less attractive to members of the electorate—will decrease turnout and make the electorate more extreme in its preferences. This result, generated by the logic of expressive incentives proposed here, is known empirically thanks to Ansolabehere and Iyengar (1995), who have shown that negative campaigns "shrink and polarize the electorate." In chapter eight, I continue my analysis of the production of mass participation with the study of producer strategies that manipulate prospective participants' *expressive* motivation. Both there, as well as here, in the analysis of instrumentally focused campaign strategy, not only will my investigation reveal the effects of either type of producer strategy on the extent of aggregate participation, and the magnitude of participants' utilities, it will also demonstrate the effects of expressively and instrumentally focused strategies on the *composition* of participants' utilities.

7.1 PRODUCER INTEREST AND PRODUCER COST

I begin by identifying the interests of producers of mass participation and the constraints under which these interests exist. In the previous chapter I have shown that conclusions drawn from the identical-preference tipping model are robust to more realistic settings of different expressive preferences for different participants, as well as an existence of both expressive and instrumentally motivated voters participating in an election. Because of this robustness, and in order to keep the analysis simple, I return whenever possible to the identical-preference tipping depictions, provided that conclusions drawn from this simplified depiction will also apply in the more realistic varied preferences cases. In addition, whenever possible, I simplify my depiction of the voters' utility curves by flattening the Y-participation curve in the original tipping figures (see figure 7.1). Because my interest is with the composition of participants' utilities—represented by the areas under the curves—this facilitates depiction. Again, the ordinal conditions of all conclusions remain unaltered by this simplification.

7.1.1 Producer Interest

In chapter six I expressed participants' utilities as:

$$u_i^x (n_x, q_i^x) = f_x (n_x) + \underbrace{p (u_i^{\Pi x} - u_i^{\Pi y}) - C_i}_{q_i^x} \qquad (7.1)$$

From this expression, and from the depiction of this relationship in figure 7.1, four different producer interests can be identified. I begin by summarizing each of these interests in analytical terms from the perspective of candidate X, and note whether the respective interest can be targeted through instrumentally or expressively focused campaign strategy. I add substantive illustration for each of these strategies in their fuller discussion that follows.

YX *Sequencing of Peaks over* n_x *(Expressive Target).* First, X-producers will strategically manipulate the location of the peak of the average voter's expressive utility curve along the n_x-dimension. As we have seen in the previous chapter, for there to be positive electoral momen-

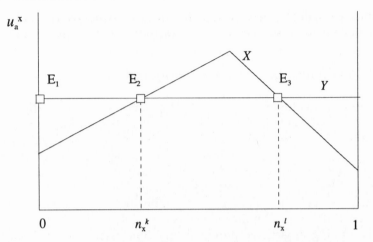

Figure 7.1: Simplified tipping depiction. In order to simplify the analysis of the composition of participants' utilities (which will be depicted as areas under the curves) the Y-participation curve has been flattened. The nature of the cross-over points, or equilibria, remains unchanged, as will the conclusions drawn from the depictions.

tum for candidate X requires that the peak of the average voter's expressive utility curve reside to the right of the average opponent voter's peak.

This sequence of locations will be a function of both f_x (n_x) and f_y (n_y): it will be a function of the expressive essence of both candidates, and thus of their expressively focused campaigning. Specifically, it will be determined by candidate-specific expressive appeal (see the description in chapter five of greater affect intensity among modern campaigns), as well as by the campaigner's strategic shielding of the *who* dimension, as previewed in earlier chapters. Both of these campaign strategies will be discussed in chapter eight.

Location of Tipping Point n_x^k *(Expressive and Instrumental Target).* A second formally-discernible strategic target is the location of the tipping point, the point of intersection between the X- and Y-voters' utility curves. As I showed in the previous chapter, this is the point the X-producer will aim to transcend for a maximum number of prospective voters, in order to attain the higher stable-equilibrium quantity E_3.

The location of this cross-over point will be a function of the shape of the curves, given by the expressive components f_x (n_x) and f_y (n_y), as well as of the curves' autonomous heights, given by the instrumental component q_i^x. Candidates' manipulation of the former will be discussed in chapter eight; their manipulation of the latter will be addressed shortly in this chapter, in my discussion of "instrumental enhancement."

Distortion of Perceived Value for n_x^k *(Expressively Determined Target).* Third, an X-producer will attempt to indicate to prospective participants what aggregate X-support levels currently are: formally, producers will not only wish to specify a tipping point, but also to convey the information—or create the illusion—that the electorate presently is to the right of that unstable equilibrium point, but also to the left of the higher-level stable equilibrium point.

This campaign strategy does not emerge directly from the expressive parameters that define the curve, but is dictated by the targeting of prospective participants' expressive motivation. It involves the X-producer's strategic positioning of alleged X-participation levels along the n_x dimension. Given its expressive base, this campaign strategy will be explored in my discussion of expressively targeted producer strategy in chapter eight.

Location of Stable-Lead Equilibrium Point E_3 *(Expressive and Instrumental Target);.* Fourth, and finally, producers will try to create a high E_3 equilibrium, which is to say they generate a high stable base of support for their own candidate. This is an elaboration of the strategic sequencing of X- and Y-utility peaks already identified. As previously noted, strategic sequencing dictates, first, that X's campaign manager will want the peak of the participant's utility curve to reside to the right of the equivalent point on the Y-participation curve. In addition, and more strongly, he will now also want the peak to take on a high value along the n_x-dimension, and the saturation-induced point of intersection to lie high on the n_x-dimension.

In chapter eight I will show how the location of the peak n_x^* and of the stable-equilibrium cross-over point E_3, will be a function of expressively focused strategy—manipulation of the *who* dimension identified previously. In addition, the location of E_3 will also be a function of instrumentally focused strategy, as I discuss in this chapter.

Because my concern in this chapter is with instrumentally focused producer strategy (and its expressive cost), I begin with the two types of campaign strategy that contain an instrumental target. In terms of equation 7.1, both of these involve a manipulation of q_i^x, or the autonomous height of the X-participation curve relative to the Y-participation curve. Such manipulation will determine the location of the unstable equilibrium point (the tipping point) and of the stable equilibrium points E_1 and E_3. As I will also show, for the producer to change the height of the curve will also determine aggregate turnout levels.

7.1.2   Producer Cost

Producers' ability to pursue these different targets using both instrumentally and expressively focused campaign strategy are subject to constraints. At a very minimum there is a cost of campaigning: most simply, making a candidate more attractive among a population is costly. More elaborately, producer costs typically will vary: for example, altering the perceived value of current support level, n_x, (the third producer target previously identified) will become more costly as the alleged level of support moves further away from true support levels. Sometimes producer costs will be financial ones. In that case, as I will show, there can be a direct, endogenously defined transfer between producers of participation and participants. At other times, the cost (or constraint) will be nonfinancial, in which case it no longer will be transferable. At that point equilibria can be identified only if we make assumptions about an exogenously defined budget constraint. In either case, costs will determine the location of the likely equilibria in our analysis, as well as the composition of participants' symbolic and instrumental utilities. As before, I begin with a pure choice-based approach assuming full participation. I subsequently introduce turnout.

Three types of instrumentally focused campaign or advertising strategies are available to the producer in his attempt to elicit greater X-participation via the targets I have identified. The first two involve the raising of the (perceived) utility associated with X-participation, and the third involves a lowering of the associated cost. Although all three strategies have identical effects on voter choice in a full-participation election, they have different effects on turnout.

7.2   Raising Benefit

7.2.1   Positive and Negative Campaigning

The first manner of raising benefit is to make a candidate or good more attractive. For Downsian spatial theorists this involves the candidates' moving along the policy spectrum to the position of the median voter, thereby maximizing across voters the sum of the distance $(u_i^{\Pi x} - u_i^{\Pi y})$ in the electoral context of equation 7.1. In the context of market consumption, equivalently, economists identify goods that reside on indifference curves that score highest in a two-good or multi-good market. In either case, prospective participants are limited by a budget constraint—*one* vote in the electoral context, *d* dollars in the market. In both cases, if producers attempt to maximize participation, they compete with one another by outscoring each other on a maximum number of participants' utility scales. And in both cases, the extent to which a single good or candidate's producer can elicit greater support is constrained by the preference heterogeneity among prospective participants (see chapters four and five). Any kind of improvement of the attractiveness of a candidate or good X will result in a *raising of the average participant's utility curve for* X.

Conversely, the same is achieved not through a strategy of positive campaigning but of negative campaigning against the opposing candidate. Negative campaigning is to reduce the utility the voter associates with voting for an opponent. In terms of our tipping model, for X to engage in negative campaigning is for him to reduce the height of the utility curve associated with participation in Y. In terms of voters' relative preferences of candidates, this is identical to the previous scenario of positive campaigning, as it involves increasing the average voter's difference between the utility associated with X and with Y. As I will demonstrate, both strategies change the locations of the tipping point and the E_3 equilibrium victory point for X. As I will also show, however, the two strategies have opposite effects on electoral turnout. It is, of course, important to note that the raising of the X-participation curve will be effective only in the presence of some noninstrumental (non-outcome-oriented) returns to participation. In the absence of such returns, *no* degree of campaigning will induce participation on strictly instrumental grounds, provided that voters are aware of the true instrumental potency of their vote. (I return to this as I introduce turnout.)

7.2.2   Exaggerating Instrumental Potency

Indeed, a second manner in which producers may enhance the participant's utility associated with her participation is by *exaggerating* the potency of her vote's effect on the collective outcome. In chapter three I showed how, in the electoral context, returns to participation were mediated by the probability of influencing the electoral outcome, *p*. The value of *p* diminishes rapidly as the size of the electorate grows larger, and as the remaining electorate's prior probability of voting for one candidate over another, in a two-candidate race, deviates further from 0.5.

In chapter four I acknowledged that voters simply may not be aware of the strong degree of irrelevance of their vote. In the same light it can be suggested that candidates will try to convince voters of how important their vote is in generating a preferred outcome. For example, in the opening illustration of this book, George Bush, at the end of a televised presidential debate, after stressing the impossibility of defeat, stressed the importance of the individual vote in securing victory. In terms of the instrumental model of returns presented by Riker and Ordeshook (1968) and others, this can be interpreted as raising a participant's perceived value for the probability of effecting the outcome p, resulting once again in an increase in voters' (perceived) value for q_i^x.

7.3 LOWERING COST

The practice of positive campaigning for one's own candidate, negative campaigning against the opposing candidate, and stressing the importance of the individual vote in getting the preferred candidate elected, all increase the difference in height between the utility curve associated with the preferred candidate over that of the trailing candidate. An identical result is obtained by indirectly raising the benefit associated with X-participation via a lowering of the cost of participation.

Targeting the cost of participation can take on several forms. First, it may involve reducing the literal cost of participation, a phenomenon witnessed primarily in the consumer market context, but also seen (to a much lesser extent) in the electoral realm. In the industrial context, returning to the history of the Cola wars, the Pepsi-Cola company, after several tries, managed to break into the soft drink market in the early 1930s by dramatically underpricing Coca-Cola. It was here that it introduced the twelve-ounce bottle for a nickel, thereby giving rise to the famous advertising slogan "Twice the Product for the Same Price." By reducing the very cost of participation, the Pepsi company raised consumers' instrumental utility, thereby inducing their greater participation, and thereby raising the X-participation curve in our depictions.

In the electoral context, the producer's targeting of prospective participants' instrumental cost can take on one of two forms. The first resembles Pepsi-Cola's strategy in that it involves raising the expected benefit of participation by reducing its *literal* cost. Yet in contrast to the private industrial context, large-scale campaigns such as those surrounding presidential elections carry only a limited history of eliciting greater participation by reducing an electorate's costs of participation: though the soft drink producer can reduce a participant's cost simply by reducing the product's price, attempts at reducing the literal cost of voting, in contrast, are quite limited. This is consistent with expectations, because there is no market link that translates the cost borne by the participant into producers' revenue: costs (the disutility of voting) and revenues (received votes) are of fundamentally different metrics and cannot directly be transferred between participants and producers.

Still, it is quite common practice in national elections (in the United States and in Britain, for example) for local organizations to offer party-sympathetic individuals transportation to the polling booth in order to raise the probability of their electoral participation. Problems here emerge from the difficulty of identifying likely supporting voters, as well as from estimating the extent to which these voters' decision to participate is actually positively influenced by the offer of transportation: it would be inefficient to offer a ride to an individual who has already decided to participate, and it would more than defeat the purpose to misidentify likely supporters and consequently offer rides to voters of the competing party.[1] Finally, in the context of national elections, facilitating access to the polling station in this manner represents an exceptionally costly strategy. Consequently, it is one that is offered not by national party-related organizations, but more commonly by local Get-out-the-Vote (GOTV) grassroot organizations consisting of township-level volunteers and the like.

A much more important form of cost reduction in the electoral context has already been touched on and involves the producer's rephrasing of the *idiom* of cost itself. As I reviewed in chapter three, Ferejohn and Fiorina argue that rather than define participants' incentives in terms of maximizing the expected benefit of participation, a more appropriate decision rule might be one revolving around prospective participants' strategic minimizing of regret. The relevant measure of the participant's utility, therefore, is not the probabilistic magnitude of the differential utilities of two competing outcomes, but the magnitude of that differential in the *contingency* of a situation wherein the individual's participation could singularly have determined the preferred outcome. Consequently, by stressing the potential for regret, producers engaged in convincing individuals to partici-

---

[1] This, incidentally, is a "sport" among British university students who frequently misidentify themselves to the opposing party's transportation squads as supporters in order to secure a free trip to the polling station. The intention is to vote for their own preferred party candidate, while at the same time taking from a true sympathizer a transportation seat and making her participation less likely. A lesson from my undergraduate education.

pate essentially adopt an idiom stressing a *high contingent opportunity cost of abstention.*

7.4 ANALYTICAL EFFECTS

The reduction of the cost of participation in X, or of making X more attractive, will raise the average participant's X-participation curve. Shifting the idiom of costs by targeting prospective participants' concern over potential regret will also raise that curve, although here we need to emphasize that it is the perceived utility that matters in determining voters' and others' participation.

Raising the X-participation curve will result in two of the producer interests identified in section 7.1. First, raising the net benefit of X relative to Y will lower the unstable equilibrium tipping quantity n_x^k in figure 7.2 and its more general depiction in figure 7.3. If there also is a strong saturation effect to the utility curve for X and, consequently, an additional cross-over stable equilibrium point E_3, then the equilibrium quantity n_x^l of aggregate participation corresponding to E_3 also will increase. Raising the X-utility curve, consequently, both reduces the

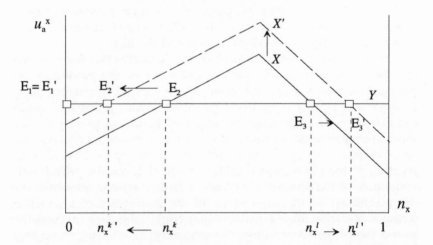

Figure 7.2: Effect of a raising of the height of the X-participation utility curve relative to the height of the Y-participation curve. (The latter is flattened to simplify illustration.) Such relative raising (1) lowers the X-tipping point from n_x^k to $n_x^{k'}$, resulting in a lower threshold of X-voting momentum; and (2) the X-leading stable equilibrium quantity from n_x^l to $n_x^{l'}$. Together, these two effects widen the "gravitational" range between the tipping point and the higher-X-support stable equilibrium.

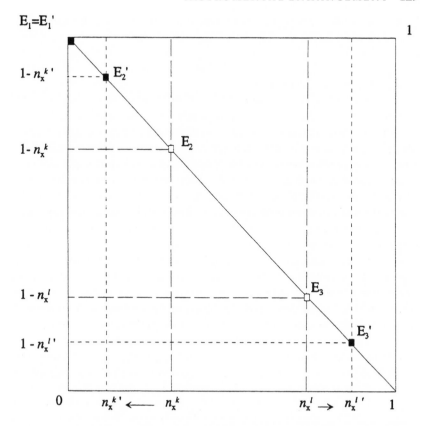

Figure 7.3: Ordinal depiction of the same conditions demonstrated in figure 7.2. If the X-participation curve intersects the Y-participation curve of figure 7.2 only once, from below, then both E_3 and E_3' will be at $n_x^l = n_x^{l'} = 1$.

"tipping" threshold to attaining higher aggregate participation levels, and raises these higher stable equilibrium participation levels themselves. The two effects together widen the band between E_2 and E_3, thereby increasing the "gravitational" range leading to the self-sustaining higher-participation equilibrium level E_3. At this immediate level, and prior to introducing considerations of turnout, all instrumentally focused strategies achieve these two producer targets.

In both figures 7.2 and 7.3, $n_x^{k'}$ and $n_x^{l'}$ represent the postenhancement values for n_x^k and n_x^l, respectively. The fact that we are dealing with a pure binary choice, full-participation model allows us again directly to map changes in either of those quantities onto corresponding changes in Y-participation levels. As before, in any bandwagon case, where the X-participation curve intersects the Y-curve only once, from underneath, the values for n_x^l and $n_x^{l'}$ remain at the (X,A) coordinates $(1,0)$.

7.5   TURNOUT AND NEGATIVE CAMPAIGNING

In chapter six I introduced into the heterogeneous-preference choice model a participant threshold u_t: if the individual voter's utility derived from an attachment to the candidate fails to outweigh her cost of participating, she will not vote for him. She may instead either vote for the other candidate or not vote at all. I reintroduce this notion of a utility threshold, as well as refer to voters with heterogeneous preferences, in order to investigate the effects on turnout of raising or lowering a voter utility curve.

Negative campaigning is for candidates to reduce the utility of voting for the opponent. In the present example, it is for candidate X to lower the Y-voting utility curve. Referring back to figure 6.5 of the previous chapter, we can analyze the effects of changing the height of a voter's preference curve for a candidate, relative to her preference curve for the other candidate. We can thus summarize the effect of a lowering of the Y-participant's curve through negative campaigning by noting (1) the tipping point n_x^k decreases in n_x; (2) the individual voter's n_x^* increases in n_x; and (3) the individual voter's n_y^* increases in n_x (which means it *decreases* in n_y). Most important, and perhaps least intuitive, (4) the utility associated with voting *at all* decreases for all equilibria, including for all the points identified in (1)-(3).

If I now reintroduce (1) the existence of voters with different utilities for X and Y, and (2) a threshold utility u_t, reflecting the minimal utility required for a voter to participate in the election, this reduced utility level for all equilibria will result in the defection of voters for whom the post-negative-campaign utility no longer clears u_t. Consequently, the decrease in utility associated with all equilibria results in a decrease in turnout. The higher a supporter's original utility curve (that is, the more extreme her support of her preferred candidate), the longer she will sustain her decision to participate on election day. Consequently, in the aggregate, we can predict that negative campaigning *polarizes and shrinks the electorate*: an increasing number of prospective voters drop out as negative campaigning continues to unfold, and the most extreme supporters will stay in the game the longest. This, of course, is the empirical finding of Ansolabehere and Iyengar (1995), and it is one that, in the present context, has been generated from the assumption that voting is expressively motivated.

If, in addition, negative campaigning makes the negative campaigner less attractive due to a "backlash" effect (for X to engage in negative campaigning relative to Y may reduce the attractiveness of X to his initial supporters), this would as a result now lower the X-curve, too. Such backlash would mitigate the predicted changes (1)-(3) above, once again moving the equilibria along the n_x-axis, this time in candidate Y's favor. However, though this would reduce the extent of the initial change in vote ratio, such backlash to negative campaigning would *further reduce turnout*: following the same logic of the utility threshold, more people would now abstain from the election, and once again the reduced remaining electorate would further be polarized.

7.6   Supply Constraints

I already noted that there will be limits to the extent to which the X-curve can be raised. These constraints emerge on the demand side in that they result from participants' preference heterogeneity, as discussed in my historical account. There is, however, an additional supply constraint in that all producers of participation will face a *cost constraint*. I approach this constraint by superimposing production costs on the participation benefit curves, thereby combining both supply and demand considerations in the same depiction.

The most important formal difference between the electoral and industrial cost settings is that production costs will be endogenous in the consumer market context: the metric of participants' and producers' costs will largely be identical. A significant part of participants' burden is the financial burden of participation that accrues to the producer in the form of revenue. In the absence of subsidy, there is, consequently, an *endogenously determined extent* to which producers can lower participants' disutility by transferring their surplus to the participants.

Production costs in the electoral case, in contrast, are *exogenous* in that the budget constraint here will be externally imposed and a function of the allocation of resources through fund-raising and the like. Unless a dollar amount is placed on (and actualized from) votes, predictions about the effect of campaigning on participation levels will remain indeterminate in the electoral setting, unless the nature of the cost constraint is specified. The two settings are sufficiently similar, however, that any conclusions drawn from the endogenous industrial context will translate into the electoral context, if framed in some simple producer cost assumptions.

I begin by assuming an efficient pricing scenario wherein the utility derived from participation is offset by its cost: the participant, therefore, receives a net utility of zero. Noting, as I did in chapter five, that the rise of the mass market was characterized by the emergence of economies of scale, the creation of a physical and informational infrastructure, and the advent of modern marketing and campaign techniques, I infer the existence of *declining average costs* over the relevant range of the production of participation. Using as an example a private-industry case with declining average cost and the existence of revenues above costs (that is, profits), I deduce costs and superimpose them on the previous depiction (see figure 7.4).

Assuming existing X-participation to be at the higher stable equilibrium level n_x^l, corresponding to the stable equilibrium E_3, the vertical

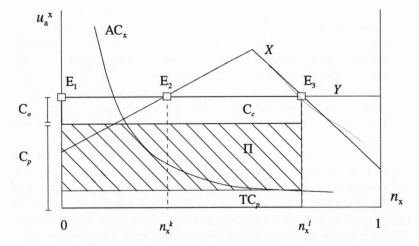

Figure 7.4: Supply-side of the production of mass participation superimposed on the demand-side tipping model. AC_x is the declining average cost curve associated with producing n_x participants. The area TC_p represents the total cost of producing n_x^l participants. The vertical height C_p represents the cost imposed on the consumer by the producer (product price in the market context, or the extent to which a candidate is able to reduce the campaign's instrumental enhancement). The area Π represents total revenue in excess of total costs, accruing to the producer (i.e., profit), and C_c defines the consumer's net burden beyond the cost imposed by the financial price. C_c is a composite of (1) participants' instrumental disutility of participation and (2) the expressive cost or benefit derived from others' participation, at n_x^l. The height of the curve at any point will therefore be determined by (1) the cost imposed on the consumer by the producer; (2) the nonfinancial instrumental cost of participating; and (3) the expressive externality of others' participation, which can be a cost or a benefit.

height C_p represents the cost imposed on the consumer by the producer. In the case of the Cola producer, that is the product's price. In the case of the electoral campaign producer, we might simply consider it to be the component of participants' literal instrumental cost that could be reduced through the producer's instrumental enhancement. Multiplying this height by the number of participants n_x^l, in the endogenous-cost industrial case, provides the sum of the areas Π and TC_p, denoting the producers' *total revenue*. Of this area, the lightly shaded region TC_p is the producers *total cost*, whereas the hashed region Π represents total revenue in excess of total costs, that is, *profits*. The most interesting area is denoted as C_c and defines the consumers' net burden beyond the cost imposed by the financial price.

C_c (or in individual terms the height C_o) is a composite of two sources of costs, one instrumental and the other symbolic. On the instrumental side, it will simply contain the nonfinancial cost of participation, the very same type of disutility attributed by theorists to participating in voting. In the endogenous-producer-cost industrial setting, it refers to the disutility of acquisition not captured by the producer in the form of revenue (for example, getting to the store). On the expressive side, the area C_c represents the expressive costs or benefits derived by participants from aggregate participation levels. As participation levels vary, the utility derived by individuals from participating also will vary. Analytically, therefore, assuming an efficient zero net-benefit scenario for the participant, the height of any point along the curve will be determined by three components: (1) the cost imposed on the consumer by the producer (that is, the price); (2) the nonfinancial instrumental cost of participating (that is, the additional effort of participation); and (3) the symbolic or expressive externality of others' participation, which can be either a cost or a benefit. In the industrial case of figure 7.4, the area C_p corresponds to (1), and the area C_c is the net of (2) and (3).

The height of the area Π represents the maximum extent to which the industrial producer of participation instrumentally can enhance the individual participant's utility without incurring negative profits. It is through such instrumental enhancement that the nature and composition of participants' utility changes.

7.7   EXPRESSIVE COSTS OF INSTRUMENTAL ENHANCEMENT

There are two types of expressive cost that are generated by the producer for the participant as a consequence of making a good, or candidate, instrumentally more attractive. The first I will call "expressive crowding out"; the other I will describe via the widely, though inconsistently, used term "commodification." Both forms involve the displacement of a participant's expressive utility by an instrumental benefit.

7.7.1 Expressive Crowding Out

Social choice and game theorists are familiar with settings in which a reduction of a good's cost results in an increase in its use and thereby its "crowding" or "congestion" (Hardin 1968). Standard examples include those of toll roads or highways, where a reduction in the price charged to motorists will result in an increase in the use of the road, up to the point at which the decrease in the individual motorist's financial cost is offset by the increase in the external costs imposed on the individual by others' participation. Where previously the individual faced a higher financial cost of participation but a lower congestion cost, a trade-off has occurred as the individual's financial cost has decreased and as this decrease is offset by the increased congestion cost. The primary change to the individual participant, therefore, lies not in the magnitude of net participation costs, but in its composition: a portion of the participant's financial cost has been replaced by an increase in the external congestion cost of others' participation. An interesting parallel can be shown to exist in the trade-off between instrumental and expressive benefits.

A producer's instrumentally focused strategy initially will raise the benefits of participation, and this will result in greater aggregate participation. If there is a saturation point to individuals' tastes for a good associated with aggregate participation levels, then the initial increase in instrumental utility will be offset by an increase in the external expressive cost emerging from the increased number of participants. As with the toll road example, therefore, the primary effect of a cost reduction is not on the magnitude of an individual participant's net utility, but on its composition. This trade-off is between two different sources of utility: the producer-induced increase in instrumental utility crowds out expressive utility. Instrumentally, there is a lower cost (or higher instrumental benefit) of participation. Expressively, the value of the good is reduced. In chapter four I defined the very meaning of a participatory good X as determined in part by the extent of its use, as a good's meaning is endogenous to the level of participation in it. Expressive crowding out, therefore, represents a phenomenon whereby the good itself becomes both less valuable to its participant and "cheaper" to acquire, as its meaning changes due to its changing degree of use. I investigate this phenomenon analytically in terms of the present depictions.

7.7.2 Comparative Statics

Assume that the producer raises the X curve to the fullest extent possible (see figure 7.5). In the simpler (endogenous-cost) market case, the financial component of participation costs is reduced by the full extent of profits, Π.

Comparing figures 7.4 and 7.5, the implementation of an instrumentally focused strategy has not altered the magnitude of participation costs if we continue to assume a flattened Y-participation curve. All equilibria will occupy the same height on the depiction's vertical utility dimension. In terms of these magnitudes alone, we would expect participants to be indifferent between an E_3 and an E_3' outcome. What participants gain in instrumental utility, they lose due to the disutility imposed by greater aggregate participation levels. In the more realistic event that Y is not expressively neutral—that is, it is not defined by a flat line—the trade-off no longer is absolute, although there still will be an extent to which the gain in instrumental utility is washed out by a loss in expressive utility.

Hence, while the magnitude of the cost of X-participation has not changed, its composition has. Figure 7.4 represents a scenario wherein participants attach a high value to X and are, therefore, willing to pay a high price for it. That price is extracted in terms of an external currency:

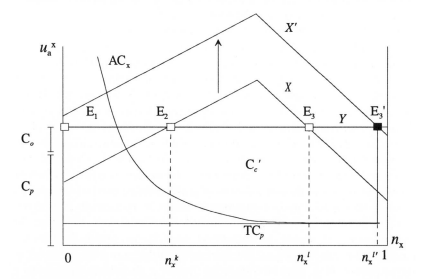

Figure 7.5: Effect of expressive "crowding out" as a consequence of an instrumental enhancement of X-participation. Participation in X increases from n_x' to n_x''. The gain in participants' instrumental utility is offset by a loss in their expressive utility.

in the case of the industrial good, this external currency is financial, and in the case of electoral and other public-good participation, it may occur in the form of the efforts associated with participation.

In figure 7.5, in contrast, while the X-curve has shifted up, say, due to a reduced cost of participating in X, X-participation itself has become *expressively* less desirable as participation levels become greater. The increase in instrumental benefit is offset—or *crowded out*—by the increased negative externality of greater participation levels. Most significantly, where previously the participant had greater utility for good X for which she was willing to pay a high price in terms of an external currency, here the increase in cost is internal: it involves a reduction in the value of X itself, as X has become cheaper. As the value of X in part depends on its normal or ordinary participation (see chapter four), the E_3' outcome in figure 7.5 involves a choice X that is both less expensive and, to the participant, less valuable than X at E_3, even if both X's, physically defined, are one and the same good or candidate.

7.7.3 Back to Bonaccorso

For an illustration of the direct relationship between participation costs and a participatory goods value, consider, once again, the story of John Bonaccorso introduced in chapter two. Bonaccorso paid a high price in order to gain a product coveted by the masses: a prime seat at the Boston Pops Fourth of July Waterfront Concert. Bonaccorso paid a price of participation in the form of an exogenous cost C_p, which in his case consisted of the efforts associated with pitching a tent at the event site well in advance of the event date. Much of this exogenous cost, as is consistent with our analytical depictions, is within the producer's reach. Consistent with my definition of Π, and consistent with my exploration of the reduction of the cost of participation, the height of Π represents the extent to which a producer can decrease a participant's cost. In Bonaccorso's case, as I noted in chapter two, the producer in fact offered to remove the height of Π from Bonaccorso's participation cost by offering him a reserved seat. Suddenly, Bonaccorso faced a situation wherein, if he were to accept the producer's offer, he would find himself with a reduced instrumental cost of participation, but also receiving an X that in terms of its meaning was now less desirable. Physically, it was the same X: event organizers guaranteed him the very seat that he was willing to purchase at great personal cost. Expressively, however, X was a different product, as consuming it at a reduced cost equated Bonaccorso's participation with everybody else's because Bonaccorso was moved to the right along the n_x-axis, thereby reducing the expressive value of X itself. Price, in this setting, is inextricably wound up with value. As Bonaccorso himself simply remarked, "If there is no price, there's no value." As even organizers made Bonaccorso's participation less costly for him, they also destroyed the value he placed in his own participation.

7.8   COMMODIFICATION

"Commodification" in the broader social science literature is an important term in that it appears in a variety of disciplines. Interestingly, it carries two exactly contradictory definitions. It originally made its appearance in social theory in volume one of Karl Marx's *Capital* (1976a). It has become common usage in the social-theory literature, well beyond Marxian circles. "Commodity" refers to the "social," "meaning-imbued," or "fetishized" dimension of an originally lifeless object. The commodity dimension is what lifts a material thing from the innate world of objects and provides it with an interpretive or subjective dimension. Commodities, in this context, define what one theorist has called "the social life of things," wherein, most frequently, the social dimension comes into play through both market and non-market exchange relationships (Appadurai 1986).

And then there is the exact opposite definition, employed in the marketing literature. In Tedlow's (1990) terms, the Pepsi-Cola company, for example, faced its problems in the late 1930s, precisely because its product was "commodified." Unlike Coca-Cola, which had meaning to its consumers, Pepsi-Cola had no image to convey, but was cheap. "Commodity," here, refers not to an object's transmission of meaning, but to its coldly pragmatic dimension. Much as the term is used by economists in the context of natural resources, commodities carry purely instrumental value: natural gas keeps us warm, water keeps us clean, and generic soft drinks satisfy our thirst and sweet tooth. None of these are significant to us beyond their instrumental or purely practical value.

In the analysis of this chapter I showed that an increase in the instrumental utility for participants will increase aggregate participation levels up to the point at which this gain is offset by the resultant loss in expressive value. Assume, instead, that producers not only raise an expressive product's instrumental benefit, but define the product itself as expressively neutral, or entirely instrumental, as they do candidate or product Y in the flat-curved depiction of figure 7.1. There is no socialized image to the good or candidate, but a great deal of information provided by the producer to the prospective participant concerning the instrumental qualities of the good or the candidate. (Analytically, here, we have returned to defining candidates much as rational choice theorists typically define them.)

There are two immediate consequences to the producer, of a flatter, low-symbol-intensity X-curve. One is that any change in X's height relative to Y will result in *greater volatility in X-participation levels*. The other is that the instrumentally determined height of the participation curve of an instrumentally defined X will quite easily by beaten by a symbol-intensive competitor. I discuss briefly both consequences here and return to them at the end of my investigation of symbolically focused producer strategy in chapter eight.

Analytically, the consequences of a flat, low-symbol intensity X-curve will be that any shift of the net benefit levels participants attribute to X will result in a much greater change in aggregate participation levels, due to the geometric effects of two intersecting curves' slopes on their points of intersection. Such volatility is familiar to scholars and practitioners of marketing. As I noted in the mass market history of the Cola wars, the Pepsi-Cola company finally managed to enter the market in the 1930s, when it dramatically underpriced Coca-Cola. Pepsi-Cola, however, nearly went bankrupt when, in 1939, a war-related sugar quota was introduced and Pepsi was forced to raise its beverages price by a relatively small margin (Tedlow 1990, 92). As is well-known to market historians, low-image brands purchased for pragmatic, instrumental, or "commodity" reasons elicit little consumer loyalty and are therefore intensely price elastic. As Tedlow notes (1990, 83): "The problem is that price-conscious consumers view the product in question as a *commodity*" (italics added):

> Price buyers are, in the unlovely term of more than one trade, "whores," since money is the only *desideratum*. Pepsi had proven by 1941 that it could build a profitable business by selling for less than Coca-Cola. But what would happen if the company was no longer able to sell twice as much as the market leader for the same price? To what extent does a consumer products company permanently taint itself by basing its appeal on the most prosaic buying motive and perhaps as a result attracting the most prosaic and least prestigious consumers?

In this context, it is interesting to remember that the last time the two Cola companies ever competed directly on the basis of price was in the 1930s. (Coca-Cola had always been unwilling to engage in price competition, even during Pepsi's aggressive phase, though it had been fairly "trigger happy" legally to defend its product image [Tedlow 1990, 90].) Not only have the two companies resisted open price competition ever since, they have been careful to frame all pragmatically defined product promotions in terms of supermarket- and other distributor-led events so as not to interfere with the image (Tedlow 1990, 61).

The lesson to be drawn by political consultants from this logic is that candidates should never campaign directly on an instrumental basis that is meaning neutral: even pragmatically oriented policy prescriptions should be enshrouded in imagery. Not only is this image and affect intensity required to overcome both voters' preference diversity and the collective action disincentives to participate (see chapter five), but an emphasis of a pragmatic or instrumental dimension also *destroys* the efficacy of an expressive campaign. This renders voters less loyal (that is, support less stable) and decreases the ability of the campaign to overcome the collective action problem. As with Bonaccorso, to reduce the cost or to raise the instrumental benefit will render participation less costly. That such enticement is made on the basis of cost, however, will render participation itself less desirable.

7.9   CONCLUSION

The investigation of this chapter provides four preliminary conclusions concerning the consequence of instrumental enhancement in the electoral context.

First, making candidates instrumentally more attractive in itself will not help them overcome the collective action problem. No matter the policy positioning or the reduction in the cost of participation, the costs of voting in strictly outcome-oriented terms will outweigh the returns to voting. Exceptions could be found if electoral candidates are successful in misleading prospective supporters to think otherwise, either by exaggerating the efficacy of the individual vote on the electoral outcome, or by exaggerating the opportunity cost of abstention.

Second, the extent to which producers of participation can raise the instrumentally defined height of the participant's utility curve is limited by the heterogeneity of prospective participants' preferences. In the absence of symbolic content, the height of the X-utility curve would solely be determined by nonexpressive utility and would thereby lose out to any competitor capable of generating an expressively shaped curve.

Third, as political scientists have shown (Jamieson 1992, 1996; Ansolabehere and Iyengar 1995), and as even the most casual observation will suggest, there is mounting negativity with which modern large-scale campaigns are carried out. Analytically, to lower an opponent's participant utility through negative campaigning will result in a decrease of turnout. Overall turnout will be reduced, and the electorate becomes more polarized. The very extent to which electoral supporters migrate away from their candidate will be much greater if their preference for this candidate is not largely expressive. Just as product brands protect their consumers' loyalty through image intensity, candidates can protect themselves from volatile swings in support levels through expressive intensity.

Fourth, and finally, as the expressive component determines the curvature of the X-participant's utility schedule, the degree of this curvature will determine the location of equilibrium participation levels, as well as the degree to which these outcomes are stable. As I now turn to discuss, it is here that producers of participation can efficiently manipulate the dynamics of collective support through a strategic targeting of prospective participants' expressive motivation.

Chapter Eight

EXPRESSIVE MOMENTUM STRATEGIES

> If you number among the few, call this number:
> 1-800-MARINES.
> *(Advertisement)*

> I'd never want to join a club that would have
> me as its member.
> *(Groucho Marx)*

IN THE LAST chapter I analyzed instances in which producers elicit the masses' greater aggregate participation by targeting prospective participants' instrumental utility. In addition to the demand-side constraints of such producer strategy, as emerge from the heterogeneity of participants' instrumental preferences, I also posited the presence of a cost constraint on the supply side. I noted that the presence of the collective action problem makes it impossible for any candidate sufficiently to raise voters' benefit curves on purely instrumental terms to elicit these voters' participation. Finally, I showed how an instrumentally focused campaign strategy will change the composition of participants' utility, thus rendering participation highly cost sensitive and volatile. Toward the end of this chapter, I will return to the observation more fully to discuss its implications for the producer of participation.

I now focus on the producer's enhancement of prospective participants' expressive utility. I primarily explore the effects of the producer's strategic manipulation of visible participation levels and frame it, once again, in the context of producer costs, as established in the previous chapter. I extend the model to show how participants manipulate both visible participation levels, and the expressive intensity of a participatory good X. I subsequently return to the observation that expressively focused producer strategy typically is accompanied by the horizontal shielding of participants, as first described in the jukebox setting of chapter two, and explored in the historical account of chapter five. As previewed there, participation, consequently, often is elicited by the producer's confrontation of the prospective participant with the *silhouette* of the masses: participants typically are informed of the masses' presence, but are shielded from its constituent identities. As I shall show, it is through the combined use of these two strategic tools that producers actively generate and harvest electoral (and market) momentum.

8.1   STRATEGIC DISTORTION OF PARTICIPATION LEVELS

We are confronted, on a daily basis, with information about how many others are allegedly engaged in a large variety of activities. Such information is provided both by producers responsible for these activities, be they presidential campaigns, product advertisers, or interest-group organizers, and by professional observers, such as pollsters, analysts, and the news media. The strong emphasis on a good's or a candidate's popular standing has caused some theorists to consider events in public life primarily to be "performances" (Deighton 1992). Rather than focus on any objective assessment of a good's qualities or a candidate's ability, collectives are provided with information about how that product or candidate is doing in the industrial or electoral market. In the very explicit version of this phenomenon, of polls tracking candidates through presidential primaries, Bartels (1988) suggests that one of the reasons the public is so attuned to performance in the context of electoral primaries, for example, is that a candidate's standing in the polls is one of the few consistent threads to electoral competitors' performance over the long-drawn-out electoral process.

Because aggregate participation levels matter in determining a prospective participant's decision to participate in an election, it is in the producer's interest to manipulate *perceived* aggregate support. For example, in January 1992, on a trip to Australia, then-president and incumbent candidate George Bush proclaimed the certainty of an electoral victory, stressing that American voters in the upcoming election would not make their electoral choice dependent upon the state of the U.S. economy.[1] Here, as is commonly the case with campaign rhetoric, the phrase "the American people know" was followed by information that may well have been news to the individual "American-people" member. Once again, the producer of participation attempts to draw individuals into participation by confronting them with the alleged opinions or activities of the larger collective. In electoral campaigns, similarly, candidates proclaim an electoral lead and the impossibility of defeat, despite opinion poll information to the stark contrary. Revelations that a candidate in fact knew of his impending demise several

[1] *New York Times*, January 17, 1990, page 1.

days before the actual election—as was allegedly the case with George Bush in 1992—are eventually relayed, without surprise or cynicism, in the postelectoral media coverage.[2]

Finally, as emerges from the historical account of chapter five, this reference to a collective of alleged supporters often is a vague one. I have noted with respect to Reagan's "Morning Again in America" campaign, for example, that the alleged presence of a large community of supporters often is implicit to campaign language, rather than an official jockeying around poll numbers (though the latter tends to punctuate the former, especially in the days leading up to an election). Consequently, part of the stylization of the model presented here comes from its transparent and unambiguous opposition of *actual* candidate support and *visible* support.

8.2   "Visible" Participation

The model first introduced in chapter six suggests that an individual participant's expressive utility is driven by actual participation levels, n_x. The assumption is a plausible one if, and only if, these levels are in fact visible to the individual participant: what matters is what prospective voters *perceive* or *assume* aggregate participation levels to be.

Visible participation levels to an extent are within the producer's strategic reach. I have noted on several occasions the tendency of campaign managers explicitly or implicitly to claim majority support for their candidate, and of product advertisers to provide information about the vast number of others supposedly engaged in consumption. Depending on the success of these producer strategies, participants may witness participation levels that are quite different from true participation levels. I consequently replace in the original equation 6.1 (and subsequently) the variable n_x with the variable n_x^v, where the superscript v reflects that we are dealing with *visible* participation levels. The level of n_x^v will be determined by numerous factors.

First, it will be a function of support levels portrayed in the media, through the publication of polls, for instance. Second, individuals will derive an estimate of candidate support by observing the behavior of people around them. To the extent that these vote intentions are visible, they can be treated as samples for the electorate at large. Third, and most important to us in the present context, perceived or visible

---

[2] The *New York Times* and *Boston Globe* reported on the day after the 1992 election that the Bush campaign had predicted defeat and had rented a room (for its postelectoral closing ceremony and concession) that was a third the size of the one it had rented in 1988.

candidate support levels will also be the strategic construct of producers engaged in distorting participation levels. If high aggregate participation makes my own participation more likely, producers will focus their strategic efforts at raising the value for n_x^v through advertising, by stressing there to be high aggregate participation levels. It is this dimension that I will formally explore in the analysis that follows in this chapter.

8.3 EXPRESSIVE ESSENCE

A second type of producer strategy is to be found in candidates' direct manipulation of their expressive essence. In chapter four I noted the central importance assigned by twentieth-century Continental social theorists and anthropologists to the role of ambiguity in determining an object's interpretive, and with it expressive, meaning. In chapter five I noted that presidential candidates will invoke symbol intensive images, where the expressive intensity in part is derived from the strong ambiguity of these images. I have also noted why such symbol-intensity will better bridge the masses' heterogeneity of instrumental preferences. In my discussion in chapter three of the incentive-based literature on collective action, I have noted why expressive returns are private and will thus sidestep the collective action problem.

An important component to this discussion is the extent to which producers of participation can determine their participatory good X's expressive intensity. What are the analytical consequences of successfully using campaign slogans like "Morning Again in America"?

Determining expressive intensity is to determine the functional form of f_x. I already noted that f_x, for a representative participant will determine a peak for an individual's utility, u_i^x, and that this peak will necessarily reside at $0 < n^* < 1$ (see section 6.1). Second, the X-specific subscript to f_x indicates that different goods will carry different levels of expressive intensity: in the product market, for example, Armani suits are more expressive than is any brand aluminum foil. In the electoral context, even Riker and Ordeshook (1968), for whom noninstrumental factors remained exogenous, acknowledged that the "civic" component to participants' utility will tend to be greater in presidential elections than, say, in the elections of local judges. In terms of this discussion, for presidential candidates to stress expressive intensity, and for soft drink producers to target image intensity, is for them to increase the responsiveness of individual participants to a participatory good X's normal, ordinary, or social use. In terms of our depictions, therefore, it is to increase the degree of curvature of the participant's utility for participation in X.

8.4 COMPARATIVE STATICS

I return to the simplified depiction of figure 8.1, which describes an average individual's choice between an expressive candidate or good X and a "neutral" alternative candidate or good Y.[3] I now assume that the participants utility u_a^x will be determined by the perceived or visible level of aggregate participation n_x^v.

Expressively focused candidates will indicate to the individual participant both the shape of the utility curve as well as the individual's (alleged) position along that curve. For the presidential candidate, constant reference to the support of the masses and other forms of indicating high participation levels will signal to the prospective participant both a bandwagon component to the preference schedule itself, as well as a specific point on that schedule.

In the previous example, George Bush noted the majority's alleged support of his candidacy, thereby attempting to infuse participation

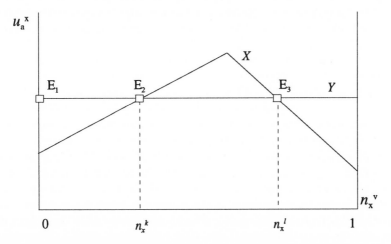

Figure 8.1: Simplified tipping depiction of participants' utilities relating *visible* participation levels and the average individual's utility derived from participating in X.

---

[3] Because, again, my analysis will involve comparing areas under the curves, I will posit this neutrality for Y. As before, for reasons spelled out in the previous chapter, all analytical conclusions are fundamentally the same as they would be if Y were an expressive choice.

with a sense of fashionability. At the same time, Bush indicated to prospective participants that they occupied a position along that implied fashionability preference schedule, and the inferred participation level was one that cleared the critical tipping quantity required for participation to increase further on its own momentum. In terms of equation 5.1, the producer's effective targeting of the preference shape will affect f_x for X, while his indicating a particular position on an individual's preference map will involve manipulating n_x^v, the visible, or perceived level of aggregate participation. Finally, any successful campaigning designed to emphasize how "meaningful" it is to be voting for one candidate or another will raise the symbol-intensity of X, and thus the magnitude of f_x.

The comparative statics of the bandwagon setting, as described in chapter five, show us that in order for the producer to change existing participation levels, he will need to move the perceived level of aggregate participation n_x^v off an equilibrium. Specifically, in our campaign and industrial examples, by indicating there to be high support or participation levels, the producer will attempt to indicate to the individual an aggregate participation level that lies beyond the unstable equilibrium quantity n_x^k, as it is any aggregate participation level beyond n_x^k that will result in the higher equilibrium participation level n_x^l. Formally, therefore, for the producer to signal high participation, in symbolic terms, is for him or her to attempt to clear the collectives tipping threshold.

8.5 NONEQUILIBRIUM OPTIMA AND GROUCHO EQUILIBRIA

In the previous chapter, using Bartels's insights into the likely nature of participants' preferences for political candidates, I noted in the example of presidential candidate Jimmy Carter in 1976 the presence of a saturation point of an individual voters' utility for these candidates, given a range of aggregate support levels. For Carter, electoral prospects became uncertain as new candidates entered the race, and the average individual's utility improved as support (measured cumulatively over time) decreased. Consequently, if the task is to enhance participation levels, the producer will attempt to convince the prospective participant not only that aggregate participation levels are greater than the tipping quantity n_x^k, but also that they are smaller than the equilibrium level n_x^l. Political campaigns will indicate to prospective participants that the electorate, as a whole, is still being drawn to the candidate. Advertisers of fashionable goods, similarly, will tell prospective consumers that there are many consumers of their good X such that $n_x > n_x^k$ but also that its value has not as yet been saturated, that the good is still *en vogue*, and that the public's attention has neither waned nor been taken hold of by some other, more fashionable, product.

In chapter six, I noted that an individual's expressive utility curve is shaped by two concerns—what the participant *is*, and what the participant *is not*. It is this condition that necessarily places the peak somewhere in the range of $0 < n_x^* < 1$. This means that expressively focused campaigning will refer not only to a collective of *attachment*, but also to one of *detachment*, or contrast.

A quite literal example of such a tactic of eliciting participation through reference to detachment is found in an advertising slogan for the Marines that reads, "If you number among the few, call this number: 1-800-MARINES." "Few," here, indicates some hypothetical nonequilibrium value $< n_x^l$, and the implied exclusivity is one that indicates to the potential X-participant a proximity to the peak of the X-participation utility curve n^*. The producer strategy of indicating an exclusion of participants while at the same time trying to elicit greater participation cleverly sidesteps a Groucho Marx effect. In terms of figure 8.1, the individual participant will now no longer find herself at the point n_x^l, wistfully looking up to the peak n^*, wishing that the club she belonged to were a tad more exclusive. Actual participation levels are, in this context, irrelevant, as the producer has taken on the role of providing such information and has made these levels his or her strategic fiction. I now turn to the role of costs in determining collective outcomes.

8.6   The Cost of Inducing Marginal Participation

Analytically, I have assumed an absence of information costs, as well as a scenario in which aggregate participation levels are perfectly visible to all potential participants. Yet as I noted in this chapter, it is often in the producer's interest to signal a value for n_x^v other than actual n_x. In order to predict a likely level for n_x^v that producers choose to indicate to prospective participants, I turn to producer costs, as I did in the context of instrumentally focused producer strategy in chapter seven. In the present context, we need to formalize the producer's cost of eliciting X-participation by using a distortionary strategy of targeting the visible level of aggregate X-participation. As before, I situate my illustration in the private industrial context, for here costs and revenues are endogenous. This allows me to predict likely outcomes, both in a profit-maximizing as well as in a participant-maximizing setting.

8.7   DISTORTION TARGETS AND CONTROLLING MOMENTUM

In the Marines example just mentioned, producers were said to indicate to prospective participants a *restrictive*, nonequilibrium number of alleged current X-participants n_x^r. In a homogeneous symbolic-preference binary-choice setting, as I formalized in chapter three, there is no real need to indicate this particular quantity. In fact, if we assume that the costs associated with distorting aggregate participation levels will increase as n_x^v increasingly deviates from actual participation levels n_x, it would be inefficient for the producer to aim for this n_x^*. It

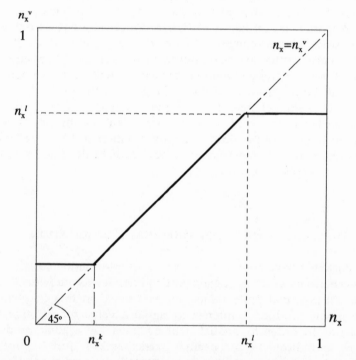

Figure 8.2: Producer's distortion target of visible participation levels. In the interval $[n_x^k, n_x^l]$, the producer of participation has no incentives to distort visible participation levels. In the interval $[0, n_x^k]$ the producer will attempt to signal aggregate participation levels n_x^k, and in the interval $[n_x^l, 1]$ the producer will signal participation levels n_x^l.

would be cheaper, and equally effective, to indicate a level of participation, just shy of n_x^l. To the extent that n_x^v is within the producer's
strategic reach, and assuming the producer engages a most efficient
strategy designed simply to elicit further participation, the producer's
likely targets for n_x^v, given actual participation levels n_x, will be as
depicted by the bold line in figure 8.2.

The producer will not attempt to distort n_x in the range between
n_x^k and n_x^l. Once aggregate participation levels transcend n_x^k, collective
participation will increase on its own momentum and then settle at
the higher equilibrium level n_x^l. Below the tipping threshold n_x^k, the
producer will attempt to inflate perceived participation levels by indicating them to be at or above n_x^k. In order to raise participation levels
beyond n_x^l, the producer will also engage in distorting aggregate participation, and this time he or she will signal a participation level shy
of n_x^l. Assuming the producer is successful in indicating aggregate
participation levels sufficient to induce greater participation (using
some distortionary strategy j), I derive the utility curve for the average X-participant in figure 8.3.

An effective distortion strategy will lead the average participant to
assume, at any time, that aggregate participation levels lie on the in-

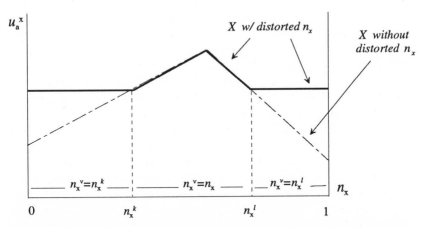

Figure 8.3: Postdistortion utility for X-participants. The outer envelope represents the X-participant's utility with an efficient distortion effort in place. In
the aggregate participation interval $[n_x^k, n_x^l]$ the representative X-participant
retains the original utility, whereas in the bordering intervals, she will receive
the utility corresponding to n_x^k-participation levels (in the $[0, n_x^k]$ interval) or
n_x^l-participation levels (in the $[n_x^l, 1]$ interval).

clusive interval between n_x^k and n_x^l. That participant's utility, therefore, is represented by the outer envelope of the X- and Y-utility curves in my previous depictions. By distorting participation levels, consequently, the producer controls electoral momentum in that he or she strategically represents a visible participation level greater than the tipping level, but smaller than the quantity n_x^l. Assuming that the producer efficiently distorts perceived aggregate participation levels over the entire range, we would expect the equilibrium outcome to be at the (X,A) coordinates (1,0). This, however, is not in itself an analytical result but represents the very definition of the efficient distortionary producer strategy as being one that draws Y-participants into the participation of X. In order to predict *actual* outcomes, I now superimpose cost constraints associated with a distortionary strategy j. It is through such cost constraint that we can conclude to what extent the producer will generate electoral momentum among prospective participants.

8.8   COST CONSTRAINTS

In the aggregate-participation range between n_x^k and n_x^l, I assume the producer does not vest any effort in distorting X-participation levels, as within that range, aggregate participation levels will increase due to the gravitational stable equilibrium characteristics of n_x^l. Above the range, the producer will face a cost of distortion as he will strategically continue to indicate aggregate participation to be at n_x^l. Because actual participation levels increase as a result of such strategic distortion, the efforts associated with indicating limited participation will also increase. If the Marines, in my previous example, are capable of eliciting greater enrollment through the signal of selective membership, then it will become increasingly difficult for the Marines to convince prospective applicants of this selectivity if a steadily increasing proportion of the population is observed joining the Marines. The costs of a distortionary strategy, therefore, increase as actual participation levels move further away from the strategic target. Similarly, in the range below the unstable equilibrium tipping level n_x^k, the producer will face a cost of distortion whereby its magnitude, too, will depend on the distance between actual participation levels n_x and strategically signaled participation rates n_x^k. For the presidential candidate to signal significant voter support, for example, will be considerably more difficult and more costly if actual support is extremely low. In figure 8.4 I infer a marginal cost of producing an additional participant via a distortionary strategy j.

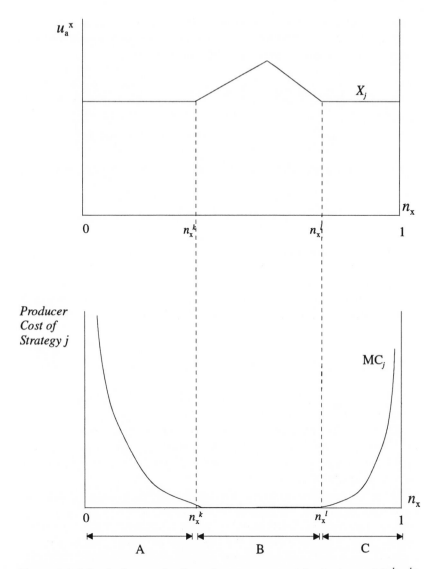

Figure 8.4: Marginal cost of a distortionary strategy j. In the interval $[n_x^k, n_x^l]$, producers will employ no distortion, and the cost of producing an additional participant will be zero. The greater the distortion (i.e., the further n_x^v moves away from actual participation levels n_x), the greater the marginal cost.

We can identify three segments to the producer's cost associated with producing an additional participant via applying an efficient strategy of distortion j. These can be summarized as:

$$MC_j = \begin{cases} g(n_x - n_x^l) & \text{if } n_x > n_x^l & \text{[range C]} \\ 0 & \text{if } n_x^k < n_x < n_x^l & \text{[range B]} \\ h(n_x^k - n_x) & \text{if } n_x < n_x^k & \text{[range A]} \end{cases} \qquad (8.1)$$

In figure 8.4, g and h describe functions for which, respectively:

$$\begin{array}{ccc} g' > 0 & \text{and} & g'' > 0 \\ h' > 0 & \text{and} & h'' > 0 \end{array} \qquad (8.2)$$

The first-order condition of both functions is positive because the marginal cost of producing an additional participant increases as actual participation levels move away from strategically targeted levels. The depiction additionally infers a positive second-order condition in that it assumes diminishing returns to the distortionary strategy j.

8.9 PROFIT VERSUS PARTICIPANT MAXIMIZATION

Finally, we are capable of predicting likely aggregate participation levels in X. I infer from the marginal cost of producing an X-participant using a distortionary strategy j, an average cost curve AC_j. I add this average cost for strategy j to the average cost of producing X, as identified in figure 5.6. I derive the depiction of figure 8.5, of producers' eliciting of participation.[4]

As in the previous chapter, the height C_p represents the price of participation, which, in the industrial context, is the financial component to the cost of participation. C_o is the nonfinancial cost of participation, and it is the sum of the disutility of participation plus the external symbolic cost or benefit of others' participation. The producer will choose to distort aggregate participation levels either until n_{MC} or n_{AC} prospective participants have been drawn into participating in X. The former aggregate-participation level is consistent with a *profit-maximizing* outcome, whereas the latter represents a zero-profit, *participant-maximizing* outcome. Therefore, depending on the desired target, the industrial producer will engage in eliciting further partici-

---

[4] For simplicity's sake, I assume that the marginal cost of X itself is zero. More realistic assumptions of a small positive marginal cost do not significantly change the figure.

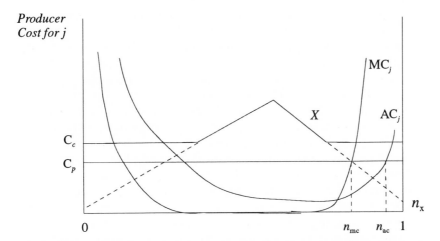

Figure 8.5: Marginal and average costs of a distortionary strategy j. The vertical height C_p represents the cost imposed on the consumer by the producer (product price in the market context, or the extent to which a candidate is able to reduce the campaign's instrumental enhancement). C_c is a composite of (1) participants' instrumental disutility of participation and (2) the expressive cost or benefit derived from others' participation. n_{mc} represents the profit maximizing quantity of producing participants, whereas n_{ac} represents the participant-maximizing quantity.

pation via a distortionary strategy j until aggregate participation levels reach one of these two levels.

In the electoral context, the producer faces the same cost constraints but here, as noted earlier, costs and revenues are *exogenous*. Consequently, as in the context of instrumentally targeted producer strategy, in order to predict precisely what likely aggregate participation levels will be, the benefit of additional votes elicited will need to be expressed in terms of revenue equivalents. More reaslistically, we need to incorporate an exogenous budget constraint. The nature of my predictions, in the electoral case, will not, however, fundamentally be any different.

8.10 Composition of Utility

In chapter six, I showed that an X-producer's attempt at eliciting greater participation in X by targeting prospective participants' instrumental motivation resulted in an increase in the number of X-participants. I also showed that this came at a symbolic cost, either in the form of "symbolic crowding out," or in the form of "commodification": more participants joined in the participation of X, though the producer-induced increase in instrumental benefit was offset by the additional cost of the greater number of X-participants. Whereas the magnitude of net benefits remained the same, the expressive value associated by the participant with the good X itself diminished. Furthermore, on the supply side, the extent to which the X-producer could raise the X-utility curve was constrained by the producers' surplus, or Π. Therefore, on the producer's side, instrumental enhancement came at a direct trade-off of producers' surplus.

The effects of an expressively focused producer strategy on the composition of participants' utility is quite different, as represented in figure 8.6.

Assuming that producers invoke collective momentum until aggregate participation levels are at the profit-maximizing producer's target quantity n_{MC} (corresponding to the producer-invoked stable equilibrium E* in the figure), the magnitudes of an individual participant's nonfinancial and financial participation costs C_o and C_p are identical to those identified in the n_x^l-aggregate-participation scenario, as shown in figure 7.6 of chapter seven. Despite the fact that n_{MC} participants participate in X, due to the producer's distortion strategy, participants themselves will perceive only an aggregate par-

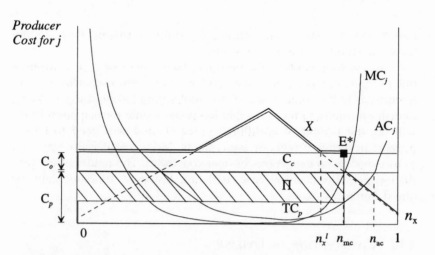

Figure 8.6: Postdistortion composition of participant utility for a profit-maximizing strategy. Participants face the same composition of utility they faced in the nondistorted stable equilibrium n_x^l-outcome (shown in, figure 7.6), although here aggregate participation levels are at n_{mc}.

ticipation level of n_x^l. Because the nonfinancial cost of participation will remain the same, and the symbolic externality to others' participation will be identical to the magnitude corresponding to an n_x^l-outcome, the aggregate of those two quantities, C_o, will also remain the same. For the individual participant, the nature and composition of utility, therefore, will be the same as in a setting in which the producer does not strategically elicit greater participation. The number of participants, however, will have increased. Compared to an instrumentally focused higher-participation setting, on the basis of the conclusion drawn at the end of chapter six, participants attach a higher symbolic value to the good X itself. Although their net benefit of participation in X remains the same (at zero, in our example), both the external cost of X, and the benefit derived from (or attributed to) X by the participant, are greater. To return once more to the example of John Bonaccorso and his Fourth of July concert, the outcome would translate into one whereby Bonaccorso is one of a large number of participants purchasing seats, but whereby Bonaccorso himself is still under the impression that his own involvement is a special one.

Finally, in the context of the jukebox model and at the end of chapter five, I noted the need of producers to shield prospective participants from the identity characteristics of their fellow participants—which I called the "Lennons" problem. Beyond some level of aggregate participation, the knowledge of *who* else is participating in a good X will become a liability. It is for this reason that product manufacturers make decreasing use of celebrity spokespersons, once they are past a point of mass participation (King 1990; Walker 1992), and that negative campaigns associate opponents with particular types of supporters.

In the semiotic terms of chapter three, shielding can be understood as a producer strategy of preserving X's polysemy or multivocality. In the formal terms noted in the beginning of this chapter, it can be understood as the producer's protection and enhancement of the symbol intensity contained in f_x. Analytically, the horizontal shielding of fellow participants preserves the symbolic shape for the average participants' utility for a participatory good X. In terms of the average participants' utility as shown in equation 8.1, the strategic shielding of fellow participants preserves the participatory good X's symbol intensity as expressed by the curvature of the symbolic function X. As I discuss in the concluding section, it is through this preservation of a participatory good's symbolic essence that producers in mass settings overcome the heterogeneity of the collective's preferences.

8.11 CONCLUSION

In part one of this book, I described the emergence of both an electoral and an industrial mass market and the changing role of producers of participation in both these realms. Where, previously, producers had limited access to a small number of prospective participants with relatively homogenous preferences, increasingly they came to be in possession of a steadily enhanced technological reach of a growing and increasingly heterogeneous group of prospective participants. As I described in both the electoral and the industrial setting, producers switched their strategy of eliciting participation to increasingly targeting the symbolic components of participants' motivation.

In this and the previous chapter, I reproduced analytically the effects of both instrumentally and symbolically focused producer strategy, both in terms of the resultant change in participation levels, and in terms of the different types of utility participants derive out of a participatory good X. I noted that producers could change the instrumental dimension of a participatory good either by enhancing its benefits to maximize the number of prospective participants, or by decreasing its cost. Alternatively, producers could manipulate a good's symbolic dimension by targeting the participatory good's meaning.

There are, typically, three components to a producer's symbolically focused strategy. To begin with, as first identified in chapter five, and approached in more formal terms in this chapter, the producer raises a good's symbol intensity by making it ambiguous. Second, the producer distorts participation levels in order to maximize the number of prospective participants drawn into participation. And, third, the producer shields the participant from the exact identity characteristics of her fellow participants.

In the context of presidential campaigns, for example, (1) the candidate employs ambiguous terms involving "Family Value," "the Flag," "Pride," and so forth; (2) the candidate will tell us that there are high (but not saturated) levels of aggregate support; and (3) he will not tell us who it is that offers such alleged support. By the same token, candidates apply the reverse on each other: George Bush, in 1988, decried in unambiguous and nonsymbolic, pragmatic terms Dukakis's alleged dangerous inexperience in foreign affairs (Jamieson 1992, 106). Furthermore, Bush insisted that Dukakis was less popular among the electorate. And, finally, the Bush campaign made an almost surreal reference to the identity characteristics of Dukakis voters by noting that convicted murderer Willie Horton allegedly told an interviewer he would vote for Dukakis if he were given the chance to participate in the election. For reasons I noted in chapter six, such negative campaigning will reduce the attacked candidate's support; it will reduce the size of the electorate; and it will polarize the electorate.

As I identified in this chapter and the last, there are a host of specific consequences both for participants and for producers that emerge from the use of an expressively as opposed to an instrumentally focused strategy.

First, as I noted in chapter seven, an instrumentally focused strategy typically involves a direct trade-off with producer profits. Graphically, I have shown that this essentially represents a transfer of benefits from producers to participants. In contrast, symbolically focused producers do not result in producers' handing their surplus to participants, but instead apply it to the strategic distortion of participation levels. Consequently, individual participants still face not only the same magnitude, but also the same type of costs that they faced in the absence of any producer intervention. In the industrial case, this additionally preserves the product's price, and the industrial producer will most likely engage in shielding until profits are maximized. In the electoral setting, where costs and revenues are exogenous, no simple profit-maximizing outcome can be derived. Yet the same constraints hold: for even if the budget constraint is an external one, resources invested in a distortionary practice, and other types of symbolically focused strategy, will be of greater efficacy in securing higher participation.

I have shown that another important difference between the effects of instrumentally and symbolically focused producer strategies is to be found in the different composition of participants' costs and benefits. As we saw in this chapter, a producer strategy of distorting participation levels results in a greater aggregate-participation outcome in which the composition of utility remains unchanged. In the instrumental context, in contrast, be it in the form of "expressive crowding out" or "commodification," the individual's attachment to the good itself will be weaker. In both cases, the very idiom of participation is formed to a greater extent by instrumental or pragmatic concerns. As I show analytically, and as is confirmed by consumption theorists, this has the effect of participation levels becoming more volatile.

CONCLUSION

IN CHAPTER THREE I quoted Albert Hirschman noting how, in his book *Exit, Voice, and Loyalty* (1970), he had allowed himself "to be imprisoned by the traditional notion that the use of voice is always costly." He continues, noting that his "case for the potential superiority of voice over exit would have been considerably strengthened" had he "realized that in certain situations the use of voice becomes acutely pleasurable and should therefore no longer be computed as a cost, but as a benefit." In this book I approached instances of voice, or what I called expression, as a benefit. I showed how such benefit arises from a symbolic dimension (chapter four), and how those attempting to elicit our participation in modern mass markets and mass elections do so by targeting our desire to express, or to use voice.

I have argued that expressive value is a social category in that it is anchored in a notion of normal use: for prospective participants to generate an interpretation of *what it means* to be joining an activity requires a notion of what those who participate in that activity are like. Following anthropologists and social theorists working on what they (and marketing experts) have called Lifestyle choices, I have shown how this notion untangles into two dimensions—the *who* and the *how many*. For these two parameters to matter, the good or the candidate must be expressively fertile in the first place. Finally, I have noted that though expressive value is socially determined in that it emerges against the backdrop of a collective's preferences, it will matter not only in public, but also in private. Being, as emerges from social context, defines the individual regardless of whether he or she is in public or alone.

In chapter five I showed how producers of participation—marketing experts and campaign managers—learned to target the expressive dimension in markets and electorates. They did so to overcome the diversity of prospective participants' preferences, as well as to draw them into the production process, so they would overcome the collective action problem. Producers in both these settings (a) increasingly needed to and (b) were increasingly able to target the expressive dimension because of the technologically determined rise of a mass market and a mass electorate. In both cases, this rise emerged initially in the form of a national infrastructure—transportation and bottling technology in the soft drink setting, a national information infrastructure in campaigning. This led to the unified phase in mass marketing and campaigning. It subsequently evolved further in both contexts, through the rise of a television-led infrastructure that had a strong elective affinity with image-intensive advertising. I also argued that the logic put forth by spatial theorists with regard to voter choice may have some relevance in the unified market (even though, as I noted several times, this alleged logic in fact worsens the collective action problem). The logic underlying choice in the expressive context, however, is a different one, as I argued theoretically in chapters three and four, historically in chapter five, and formally in chapters six, seven, and eight.

In building this approach, it was necessary to involve several different methodological orientations and draw from several social science disciplines. Undoubtedly, and unavoidably, this risks a heavily stylized relationship of the argument with any one discipline. But despite this methodological flattening, my hope is that a larger argument has emerged: to understand Choice requires that we understand several motivational dimensions simultaneously.

First, we require an individual-level behavioral assumption, one that is anchored in a social or psychological theory. I drew on a former, though it frequently made implications of a latter. Because I tried to highlight the presence of an "existential" basis to Choice, I suspect a richer argument still could have been attained by more explicitly drawing on schools of psychology and psychoanalysis.

Second, we need to be explicit about the relationship between the individual and the collective. Two relationships matter here, one substantive and one substantive/methodological. On the purely substantive side, tastes, preferences, and beliefs emerge from social context— hence individuals' preferences will to some extent emerge from the aggregate level: it is a perception of a collective that will determine an individual's preferences. At the same time, collective behavior emerges from an aggregation of individuals' behavior (where this individual-level behavior itself is based on individuals' preferences and beliefs). All equilibria implied in the theoretical chapters and presented in the simplified context of the tipping models are the result simultaneously of these macro-to-micro and the micro-to-macro dimensions. These are "social" equilibria.

Third, we need to be explicit about the nature of rationality underlying choice and must also allow for different rational motivations to exist simultaneously. I have done this in two different ways. First, participants in my approach were primarily driven by expressive concerns. Producers of participation, in contrast, were motivated by outcome-oriented instrumental concerns, such as participant maximization. Pursuing these *instrumental* concerns involved targeting participants' *noninstrumental* motivation. Second, I allowed for the interplay of different motivations in my formal approach. In constructing the tipping models, I paid particular attention at every point to the robustness of my predictions to settings wherein not all participants were expressively motivated, or at least were not identically so. This made for tedious analysis, but curtailed the extent to which the standard rational choice assumption of narrowly instrumental rationality was swept aside by a single, equally stylized and homogenized alternative assumption.

Finally, a question that remains is where this type of approach should go from here. In addition to developing greater "inward" sophistication—notably by expanding on its theoretical foundation and by improving its formal modeling of expressively driven behavior—there is need for a sophisticated "outward"-oriented applied dimension. For reasons I noted in chapter six, a statistical investigation of the endogeneity of the macro- and microlevel is extremely difficult. Such an investigation requires estimations such as whether polls, which measure individuals' opinions, also determine these opinions. As I also noted, two promising developments may help us break out of this endogeneity. They are to be found, first, in experimental research and, second, in recent advances in statistical techniques, capable of drawing microlevel inferences from aggregate-level measurement (known as "ecological" inference). Both of these represent research areas I have begun to work in.

Finally, a larger issue I have tried to argue for is the careful breaking down of barriers that separate economic, rational, social, and public choice approaches from those characteristically pursued by social and political theorists, anthropologists, psychologists, and philosophers. The differences are primarily methodological in origin—as most concerned appear to agree—but not competingly so—as most concerned appear to overlook. Very crudely put, the former group is where we should turn to aggregate or systematize individual-level preferences in order to understand how collectives operate. The latter group can teach us where these preferences come from in the first place. In this book I have tried to present an example for the type of investigation we can pursue if we turn to both types of social science simultaneously.

REFERENCES

Akerlof, George. 1984. *An Economic Theorist's Book of Tales: Essays that Entertain the Consequences of New Assumptions in Economic Theory*. New York: Cambridge University Press.

Aldrich, John H. 1997. "When is it Rational to Vote?" In *Perspectives on Public Choice*, ed. Dennis C. Mueller. New York: Cambridge University Press.

Alvarez, R. Michael, and Jonathan Nagler. 2000. "Should I Stay Or Should I Go? Sincere and Strategic Crossover Voting in California Assembly Races." In *California's Open/Blanket Primary: A Natural Experiment in Election Dynamics*, ed. Bruce E. Cain and Elisabeth R. Gerber. Berkeley, Calif.: IGS Press.

Ansolabehere, Stephen, and Shanto Iyengar. 1995. *Going Negative: How Political Advertisements Shrink and Polarize the Electorate*. New York: Free Press.

Appadurai, Arjun, ed. 1986. *The Social Life of Things: Commodities in Cultural Perspective*. New York: Cambridge University Press.

Barry, Brian, and Russell Hardin, eds. 1982. *Rational Man and Irrational Society? An Introduction and Sourcebook*. Beverly Hills: Sage.

Bartels, Larry. 1988. *Presidential Primaries and the Dynamics of Public Choice*. Princeton, N.J.: Princeton University Press.

Barthes, Roland. 1988. *The Semiotic Challenge*. New York: Hill and Wang.

Berry, Jeffrey M. 1989. *The Interest Group Society*. Glenview, Ill.: Scott, Foresman.

Bikhchandani, Sushil, David Hirshleifer, and Ivo Welch. 1992. "A Theory of Fads, Fashion, Custom, and Cultural Change as Informational Cascade." *Journal of Political Economy* 100(5): 992–1026.

Boddewyn, J. J., and Katherin Marton. 1978. *Comparison Advertising: A Worldwide Study*. New York: Hastings House.

Bourdieu, Pierre. 1984. *Distinction: A Social Critique of the Judgement of Taste*. Cambridge, Mass.: Harvard University Press.

Brams, Steven J., and Morton D. Davis. 1982. "Optimal Resource Allocation in Presidential Primaries." *Mathematical Social Sciences* 3: 373–388.

Brennan, Geoffry, and James Buchanan. 1984. "Voter Choice: Evaluating Political Alternatives." *American Behavioral Scientist* 28(2): 185–201.

Brennan, Geoffry, and Loren Lomasky. 1993. *Democracy and Decision: The Pure Theory of Electoral Preference*. New York: Cambridge University Press.

Buchanan, James M., and Gordon Tullock. 1962. *The Calculus of Consent: Logical Foundations of Constitutional Democracy*. Ann Arbor: University of Michigan Press.

Cantril, Albert Hadley. 1991. *The Opinion Connection: Polling, Politics, and the Press*. Washington, D.C.: Congressional Quarterly.

Chamberlin, John. 1974. "Provision of Collective as a Function of Group Size." *American Political Science Review* 68, (2): 707–16.

Chwe, Michael Suk-Young. 2001. *Rational Ritual: Culture, Coordination, and Common Knowledge*. Princeton, N.J.: Princeton University Press.

Cleary, David P. 1981. *Great American Brands: The Success Formulas That Made Them Famous.* New York: Fairchild.

Cohen, Richard. 1985. "Criticizing Single Mothers." *Washington Post,* July 16, 1993.

Cox, Gary. 1997. *Making Votes Count: Strategic Coordination in the World's Electoral Systems.* New York: Cambridge University Press.

Crisp, Quentin. 1987. *The Wit and Wisdom of Quentin Crisp.* New York: St. Martin's Press.

Dahl, Robert Alan. 1963. *A Preface to Democratic Theory.* Chicago: University of Chicago Press.

Dannen, Fredric. 1990. *Hit Men: Power Brokers and Fast Money Inside the Music Business.* New York: Times Books.

David, P. 1985. "Clio and the Economics of QWERTY." *American Economic Review: Papers and Proceedings* 75: 332–37.

Deighton, John. 1992. "The Consumption of Performance." *Journal of Consumer Research* (December): 362–72.

Denzau, Arthur D., and Douglass C. North. 1994. "Shared Mental Models: Ideologies and Institutions." *Kyklos* 47(1): 3–31.

Diamond, Edwin, and Stephen Bates. 1993. *The Spot: The Rise of Political Advertising on Television.* 3rd ed. Cambridge, Mass.: MIT Press.

Downs, Anthony. 1957. *An Economic Theory of Democracy.* New York: Harper.

Durkheim, Emile. 1960. *The Division of Labor in Society.* Glencoe, Ill.: Free Press.

Eco, Umberto. 1976. *Theory of Semiotics.* Bloomington: Indiana University Press.

Edelman, Murray. 1988. *Constructing the Political Spectacle.* Chicago: University of Chicago Press.

Edward, F. McQuarrie. 1992. "On Resonance: A Critical Pluralistic Inquiry into Advertising Rhetoric." *Journal of Consumer Research* 19(2): 180–97.

Elster, Jon. 1989. "Social Norms and Economic Theory." *Journal of Economic Perspectives* 3, no. 4: 99–117.

Enelow, James M., and Melvin J. Hinich. 1984. *The Spatial Theory of Voting: An Introduction.* New York: Cambridge University Press.

Erickson, Gary M. 1992. "Empirical Analysis of Closed-Loop Duopoloy Advertising Strategies." *Management Science* 38(12): 1732–49.

Ferejohn, John, and Morris Fiorina. 1974. "The Paradox of Not Voting: A Decision Theoretic Analysis." *American Political Science Review* 68(2): 525–36.

———. 1975. "Closeness Counts Only in Horseshoes and Dancing." *American Political Science Review* 96(3): 920–25.

Fiorina, Morris P. 1990. "Information and Rationality in Elections." In *Information and the Democratic Process,* ed. John Ferejohn and James Kuklinski. Urbana: University of Illinois Press.

Forkan, James P. 1980. "Pepsi Generation Bridges Two Decades." *Advertising Age,* May 5, 1980 pp. 41–43.

Frank, Robert H. 1985. *Choosing the Right Pond: Human Behavior and the Quest for Status.* New York: Oxford University Press.

Frazer, James George. [1922] 1940. *The Golden Bough.* New York: Macmillan.

Frisch, Max. 1968. *Mein Name sei Gantenbein*. Frankfurt a. M.: Fischer Bücherei.

Gadamer, Hans Georg. 1975. *Truth and Method*. New York: Seabury Press.

———. 1976. *Philosophical Hermeneutics*. Berkeley: University of California Press.

Gail, Tom. 1992. "The Use of Created versus Celebrity Spokesperson in Advertisements." *Journal of Consumer Marketing* (Fall): 15–51.

Geertz, Clifford. 1973. *The Interpretation of Cultures: Selected Essays*. New York: Basic Books.

Gellner, Ernest. 1985. *Relativism and the Social Sciences*. Cambridge: Cambridge University Press.

———. 1987. "Disenchantment with Disenchantment." In *Culture, Identity, and Politics*. New York: Cambridge University Press.

Giddens, Anthony. 1982. *Profiles and Critiques in Social Theory*. Berkeley: University of California Press.

———. 1991. *Modernity and Self-Identity: Self and Society in the Late Modern Age*. Stanford, Calif.: Stanford University Press.

Ginsberg, Benjamin. 1989. "How Polling Transforms Public Opinion." In *Manipulating Public Opinion: Essays on Public Opinion as a Dependent Variable*, ed. Michael Margolis and Gary A. Mauser. Pacific Grove, Calif.: Brooks.

Glazer, Amihai, Bernard Grofman, and Guillermo Owen. 1992. "A Formal Model of Group-Oriented Voting." Unpublished paper, University of California, Irvine.

Godwin, R. Kenneth, and Robert Cameron Mitchell. 1984. "The Implications of Direct Mail for Political Organizations." *Social Science Quarterly* 65(3): 829–39.

Goffman, Erving. 1971. *The Presentation of Self in Everyday Life*. Harmondsworth: Penguin.

Goldenberg, Edie N., and Michael W. Traugott. 1984. *Campaigning for Congress*. Washington, D.C.: CQ Press.

Goodin, R. E., and K. W. S. Roberts. 1975. "The Ethical Voter." *American Political Science Review* 69(3): 926–28.

Gottlieb, Anthony. 1993. "Review of Robert Nozick's *The Nature of Rationality*." *New York Times Book Review*, August 22.

Graber, Doris. 1997. *Mass Media and American Politics*. 5th ed. Washington, D.C.: CQ Press.

Grofman, Bernard. 1983. "Models of Voter Turnout: A Brief Idiosyncratic Review." *Public Choice* 41(1): 55–61.

Habermas, Jurgen. 1984–87. *The Theory of Communicative Action*. Boston: Beacon Press.

Hansen, John Mark. 1985. "The Political Economy of Group Membership." *American Political Science Review* 79(1): 79–96.

Hardin, Garrett. 1968. "The Tragedy of the Commons." *Science* 162:1243–48.

Hardin, Russell. 1982. *Collective Action*. Baltimore: The Johns Hopkins University Press.

Harrington, Joseph E. Jr. 1993. "Electoral Selection and the Survival of Ideologues." Unpublished paper, The Johns Hopkins University.

Harrington, Joseph E., Jr., and Gregory D. Hess. 1993. "A Theory of Campaign Strategy." Unpublished paper, May, The Johns Hopkins University.

Haug, Wolfgang. 1986. *Critique of Commodity Aesthetics: Appearance, Sexuality, and Advertising in Capitalist Society*. Minneapolis: University of Minnesota Press.

Herbst, Susan. 1993. *Numbered Voices: How Opinion Polling Has Shaped American Politics*. Chicago: University of Chicago Press.

Hirschman, Albert O. 1970. *Exit, Voice, and Loyalty: Responses to Decline in Firms, Organizations, and States*. Cambridge, Mass., Harvard University Press.

———. 1971a. *A Bias for Hope: Essays on Development and Latin America*. New Haven, Conn.: Yale University Press.

———. 1971b. "Economics and Possibilisms." In *A Bias for Hope: Essays on Development and Latin America*. New Haven, Conn.: Yale University Press.

Hirshleifer, David. 1995. "Social Influence, Fads, and Informational Cascades." In *The New Economics of Human Behavior*, ed. Mariano Tommasi and Kathryn Ierulli. Cambridge: Cambridge University Press.

Homans, George C. 1992. *The Human Group*. New Brunswick, N.J.: Transaction.

Hotelling, Harold. 1990. *The Collected Economic Articles of Harold Hotelling*. New York: Springer Verlag.

Jaben, Jan. 1992. "Negative Attacks on the Rise: Microsoft's Ads Highlight New Prominence of Negative Marketing in Business." *Business Marketing*, September, 28–32.

Jamieson, Kathleen Hall. 1992. *Dirty Politics: Deception, Distraction, and Democracy*. New York: Oxford University Press.

———. 1996. *Packaging the Presidency: A History and Criticism of Presidential Campaign Advertising*. 3rd ed. New York: Oxford University Press.

Jay, Martin. 1996. *The Dialectical Imagination: A History of the Frankfurt School and the Institute of Social Research, 1923–1950*. Berkeley: University of California Press.

Johnson, James. 1993. "Is Talk Really Cheap? Prompting Conversation between Critical Theory and Rational Choice." *American Political Science Review* 87(1): 74–86.

Kelman, Steven. 1987. "'Public Choice' and Public Spirit." *Public Interest* 87: 80–94.

King, Gary. 1997. *A Solution to the Ecological Inference Problem: Reconstructing Individual Behavior from Aggregate Data*. Princeton, N.J: Princeton University Press.

King, Thomas R. 1990. "For Colas, the Fault Is in Too Many Stars." *Wall Street Journal*, January 24.

Konrad, Walecia. 1990. "The Real Thing Is Getting Real Aggressive." *Business Week*, November 26, pp. 94, 96, 100, 104.

Ledyard, John O. 1984. "The Pure Theory of Large Two-Candidate Elections." *Public Choice* 44:7–41.

Leibenstein, Harvey. 1950. "Bandwagon, Snob, and Veblen Effects in the Theory of Consumers' Demand." *Quarterly Journal of Economics* 64(2): 183–207.

———. 1976. *Beyond Economic Man: A New Foundation for Microeconomics*. Cambridge, Mass.: Harvard University Press.

Lipovetsky, Gilles. 1994. *The Empire of Fashion: Dressing Modern Democracy.* Princeton, N.J.: Princeton University Press.

Lohmann, Susanne. 1991a. "Information Aggregation through Costly Political Action." Research Paper 1130a, Graduate School of Business, Stanford University.

———. 1991b. "A Welfare Analysis of Political Action." Research Paper No. 1132, Graduate School of Business, Stanford University.

Lowry, Robert C. 1993. "The Political Economy of Environmental Citizen Groups." Ph.D. dissertation, Kennedy School of Government, Harvard University.

Mackie, Thomas, and Richard Rose. 1997. *International Almanac of Electoral History.* 3ʳd ed. Washington, D.C.: Congress Quarterly.

Magiero, Marcy. 1993. "Lipton Tea Leaves Snapple Smarting." *Advertising Age,* November, p. 48.

Marx, Karl. 1976a. *Capital: A Critique of Political Economy.* New York: Penguin Books.

———. 1976b. *Preface and Introduction to a Contribution to the Critique of Political Economy.* Peking: Foreign Languages Press.

Mauss, Marcel. 1967. *The Gift: The Form and Reason for Exchange in Archaic Societies.* New York: Norton.

McKelvey, Richard D. 1979. "General Conditions for Global Intransitivities in Formal Voting Models." *Econometrica* 47: 1085–112.

Mickelson, Sig. 1989. *From Whistle Stop to Sound Bite: Four Decades of Politics and Television.* New York: Praeger.

Mitchell, William C., and Micheal C. Munger. 1991. "Economic Models of Interest Groups: Introductory Survey." *American Journal of Political Science* 35(2): 512–46.

Morton, Rebecca. 1991. "Groups in Rational Turnout Models." *American Journal of Political Science* 35: 758–76.

Muris, Timothy, David Scheffman, and Pablo Spiller. 1993. *Strategy, Structure and Antitrust in the Carbonated Soft-Drink Industry.* Westport, Conn.: Quorum Books.

Noelle-Neumann, Elisabeth. 1993. *The Spiral of Silence: Public Opinion, Our Social Skin.* 2nd ed. Chicago: University of Chicago Press.

Nozick, Robert. 1993. *The Nature of Rationality.* Princeton, N.J.: Princeton University Press.

Olson, Mancur. 1965. *The Logic of Collective Action.* Cambridge, Mass.: Harvard University Press.

Page, Benjamin. 1976. "The Theory of Political Ambiguity." *American Political Science Review* 70(3): 742–52.

Penubarti, Mohan, and Alexander A. Schuessler. 1999. "Inferring Micro- from Macrolevel Change." Working paper, NYU Politics Center, New York.

Popkin, Samuel L. 1991. *The Reasoning Voter: Communication and Persuasion in Presidential Campaigns.* Chicago: University of Chicago Press.

Rasmusen, Eric. 1989. *Games and Information: An Introduction to Game Theory.* Cambridge, Mass.: Blackwell.

Riker, William, and Peter Ordeshook. 1968. "A Theory of the Calculus of Voting." *American Political Science Review* 62(1): 25–42.

Rosenstone, Steven J., and John Mark Hansen. 1993. *Mobilization, Participation, and Democracy in America.* New York, Macmillan.

Sabato, Larry J. 1981. *The Rise of Political Consultants: New Ways of Winning Elections.* New York: Basic Books, Inc.

Samuelson, Paul A. 1954. "The Pure Theory of Public Expenditure." *Review of Economics and Statistics* 36 (November): 387–90

———. 1955. "Diagrammatic Exposition of a Theory of Public Expenditure." *Review of Economics and Statistics* 37 (November): 350–56

———. 1958. "Aspects of Public Expenditure Theories." *Review of Economics and Statistics* 40 (November): 332–38

Schelling, Thomas. 1978. *Micromotives and Macrobehavior.* New York: Norton.

Scherer, F. M., and David Ross. 1990. *Industrial Market Structure and Economic Performance.* 3rd ed. Boston: Houghton Mifflin.

Schuessler, Alexander A. 1999. "Ecological Inference." *Proceedings of National Academy of Sciences* 96: 10578–81.

———. 2000. "Expressive Voting." *Rationality and Society* 12(1): 87–119.

Shepsle, Kenneth A. 1972. "The Strategy of Ambiguity: Uncertainty and Electoral Competition." *American Political Science Review* 66(2): 555–68.

———. 1979. "Institutional Arrangements and Equilibrium in Multidimensional Voting Models." *American Journal of Political Science* 23: 27–59.

———. 1989. "Studying Institutions: Some Lessons from the Rational Choice Approach." *Journal of Theoretical Politics* 1(2): 131–47

———. 1991. *Models of Multiparty Electoral Competition.* New York: Harwood.

Shepsle, Kenneth A., and Mark S. Bonchek. 1997. *Analyzing Politics: Rationality, Behavior, and Institutions.* New York: W. W. Norton.

Shepsle, Kenneth A., and Barry R. Weingast. 1981. "Structure-Induced Equilibrium and Legislative Choice." *Public Choice* 37: 503–19.

Simmel, Georg. 1964. *The Sociology of Georg Simmel.* New York: Free Press.

Skinner, Quentin, ed. 1985. *The Return of Grand Theory in the Human Sciences.* New York: Cambridge University Press.

Solow, Robert. 1967. "The New Industrial State or Son of Affluence." *Public Interest* 9: 100–8.

Sperber, Dan. 1975. *Rethinking Symbolism.* Cambridge: Cambridge University Press.

Steward, David. W. 1992. "Speculation on the Future of Advertising Research." *Journal of Advertising* 21: 1–18.

Stigler, George. 1974. "Free Riders and Collective Action: An Appendix to Theories of Economic Regulation." *Bell Journal of Economics and Management Science* 5(2): 359–65.

Tedlow, Richard S. 1990. *New and Improved: The Story of Mass Marketing in America.* New York: Basic Books.

Tirole, Jean. 1988. *The Theory of Industrial Organization.* Cambridge, Mass.: MIT Press.

Truman, David B. 1951. *The Governmental Process: Political Interests and Public Opinion.* New York: Knopf.

Tullock, Gordon. 1966. "Information without Profit." *Papers on Non-Market Decision Making* 1: 141–60.

Turner, Victor Witter. 1967. *The Forest of Symbols: Aspects of Ndembu Ritual.* Ithaca, N.Y.: Cornell University Press.

Uhlaner, Carole J. 1989. "'Relational Goods and Participation: Incorporating Sociability into a Theory of Rational Action." *Public Choice* 62(3): 255–85.

Verba, Sidney, and Norman H. Nie. 1972. *Participation in America: Political Democracy and Social Equality.* New York: Harper and Row.

Verba, Sidney, Kay Lehman Schlozman, and Henry E. Brady. 1995. *Voice and Equality: Civic Voluntarism in America.* Cambridge, Mass.: Harvard University Press.

Wagner, Richard E. 1966. "Pressure Groups and Political Entrepreneurs: A Review Article." *Papers on Non-market Decision Making* 1: 161–70.

Walker, Jack L. 1991. *Mobilizing Interest Groups in America: Patrons, Professions, and Social Movements.* Ann Arbor: University of Michigan Press.

Walker, Mary. 1992. "Celebrity Endorsers: Do You Get What You Paid For?" *Journal of Consumer Marketing* 9(2): 69–76.

Walzer, Michael. 1983. *Spheres of Justice: A Defense of Pluralism and Equality.* New York: Basic Books.

Weber, Max. 1978. *Economy and Society: An Outline of Interpretive Sociology.* Berkeley: University of California Press.

West, Darrell M. 1997. *Air Wars: Television Advertising in Election Campaigns, 1952–1996.* Washington, D.C.: Congressional Quarterly.

Wright, Gerald C. 1990. "Misreports of the Vote in the 1988 NES Senate Election Study." *Legislative Studies Quarterly* 15 (November): 543–63.

———. 1992. "Reported versus Actual Vote: There Is a Difference and It Matters." *Legislative Studies Quarterly* 17 (February) :131–42.

———. 1993. "Errors in Measuring Vote Choice in the National Election Studies, 1952–88." *American Journal of Political Science* 37 (February): 291–316.

Zaller, John R. 1992. *The Nature and Origins of Mass Opinion.* New York: Cambridge University Press.

INDEX